SASKATCHEWAN HOMESTEAD

J Ken Mullen

Book Three

1932–1939

SEC.23,TP.43,RGE.21,W.2

THE HOMESTEADERS ARE MAKING A STAND
AS THE DEPRESSION IS UPON THE LAND
THE CROPS ARE NOT GOOD, THE PRICES LOW
SOME WILL HAVE TO GIVE UP, WE KNOW
THE TOUGH WILL STAY AND WORK THE SOD
THE REST THEY WILL LEAVE UP TO GOD.

J. KEN MULLEN

Note for Librarians: A cataloguing record for this book is available from Library and Archives Canada at www.collectionscanada.ca/amicus/index-e.html
ISBN 1-4251-0212-3

Printed in Victoria, BC, Canada. Printed on paper with minimum 30% recycled fibre.
Trafford's print shop runs on "green energy" from solar, wind and other environmentally-friendly power sources.

TRAFFORD PUBLISHING
Offices in Canada, USA, Ireland and UK

Book sales for North America and international:
Trafford Publishing, 6E–2333 Government St.,
Victoria, BC V8T 4P4 CANADA
phone 250 383 6864 (toll-free 1 888 232 4444)
fax 250 383 6804; email to orders@trafford.com
Book sales in Europe:
Trafford Publishing (UK) Limited, 9 Park End Street, 2nd Floor
Oxford, UK OX1 1HH UNITED KINGDOM
phone 44 (0)1865 722 113 (local rate 0845 230 9601)
facsimile 44 (0)1865 722 868; info.uk@trafford.com
Order online at:
trafford.com/06-1969

10 9 8 7 6 5 4 3 2

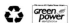

Dedication

Although the J. Mullen family and many friends actually lived, this novel about them necessitated a few additional characters to fill in the blanks where people probably existed but have been forgotten. Most of the conversation is made up. Most of the stories took place. This work is dedicated to the real people, relatives and friends of the Mullens. They left a precious legacy toward the growth of the Canadian prairies and should be remembered.

I have done the best I can to relate the stories that I heard and from the few notes written in a hospital in the last few weeks of John Mullen's life on earth. No offence is meant to anyone. This is just the way I saw their lives unfold as homesteaders.

JKM

SASKATCHEWAN HOMESTEAD

BOOK THREE

1932 - 1939

SEC.23,TP.43,RGE.21,W.2

THE HOMESTEADERS ARE MAKING A STAND
AS THE DEPRESSION IS UPON THE LAND
THE CROPS ARE NOT GOOD, THE PRICES LOW
SOME WILL HAVE TO GIVE UP, WE KNOW
THE TOUGH WILL STAY AND WORK THE SOD
THE REST THEY WILL LEAVE UP TO GOD.

JKM

Prologue

This will be a review of the two books before.

BOOK ONE 1920 - 1924

John and Florence Mullen moved out to Saskatchewan from Nova Scotia to start homesteading. There are many stories of the new type of life that they were to live. In 1921 they had a daughter Helen and in 1924 a second daughter Flo. They built their first house and started clearing land so they could plant crops.

BOOK TWO 1924 - 1932.

They started their first land breaking. and in 1925 seeded their first crop. Another daughter Aileen was born in 1926. In 1929 they bought a big tractor for breaking land. They had a son, Ken who was born in 1931.

JOHN FREEMAN MULLEN
CIRCA 1919
1896 - 1967

FLORENCE BELLE MULLEN

CIRCA 1919

1893 - 1980

SASKATCHEWAN CANADA.

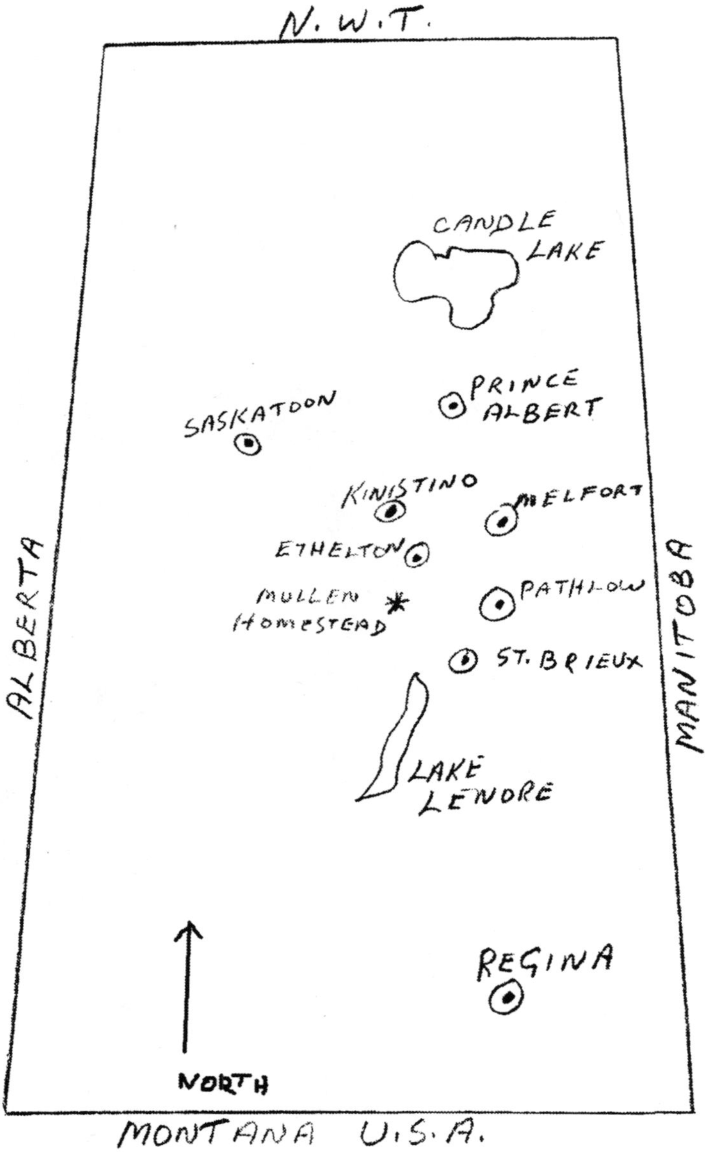

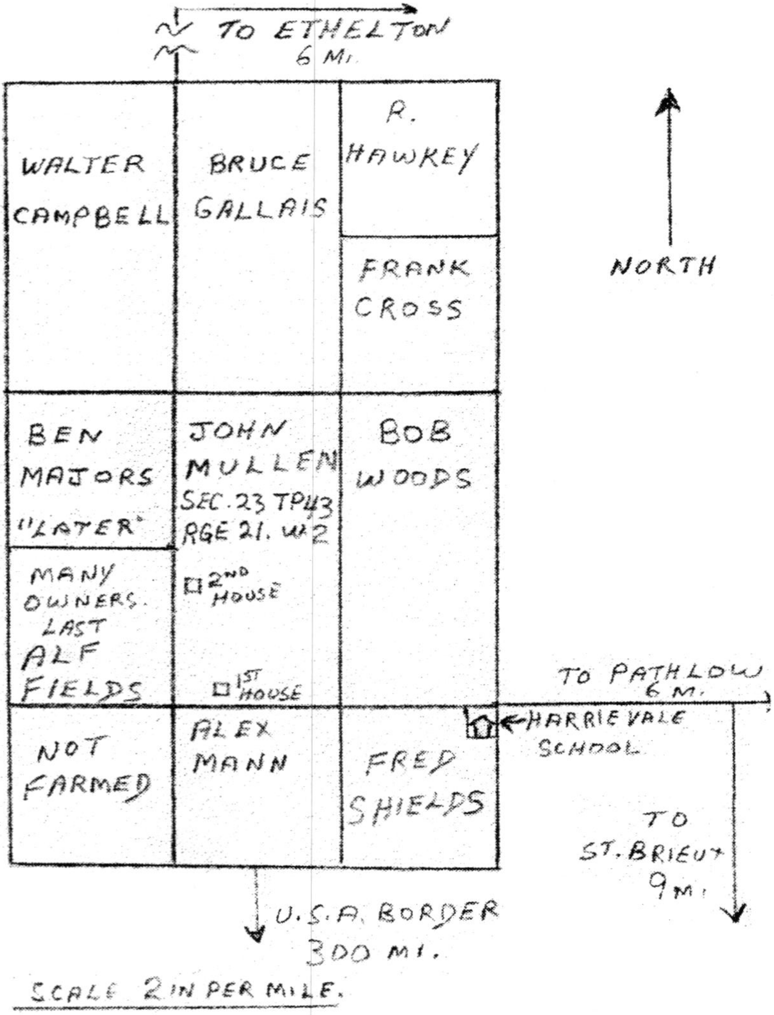
TO ETHELTON
6 MI.
WALTER CAMPBELL
BRUCE GALLAIS
R. HAWKEY
FRANK CROSS
NORTH
BEN MAJORS "LATER"
JOHN MULLEN
SEC. 23 TP43
RGE 21. W2
BOB WOODS
MANY OWNERS. LAST ALF FIELDS
2ND HOUSE
1ST HOUSE
TO PATHLOW
6 M.
HARRIEVALE SCHOOL
NOT FARMED
ALEX MANN
FRED SHIELDS
TO ST. BRIEUX
9 MI.
U.S.A. BORDER
300 MI.
SCALE 2 IN PER MILE.

HOMSTEADERS EQUIPMENT.

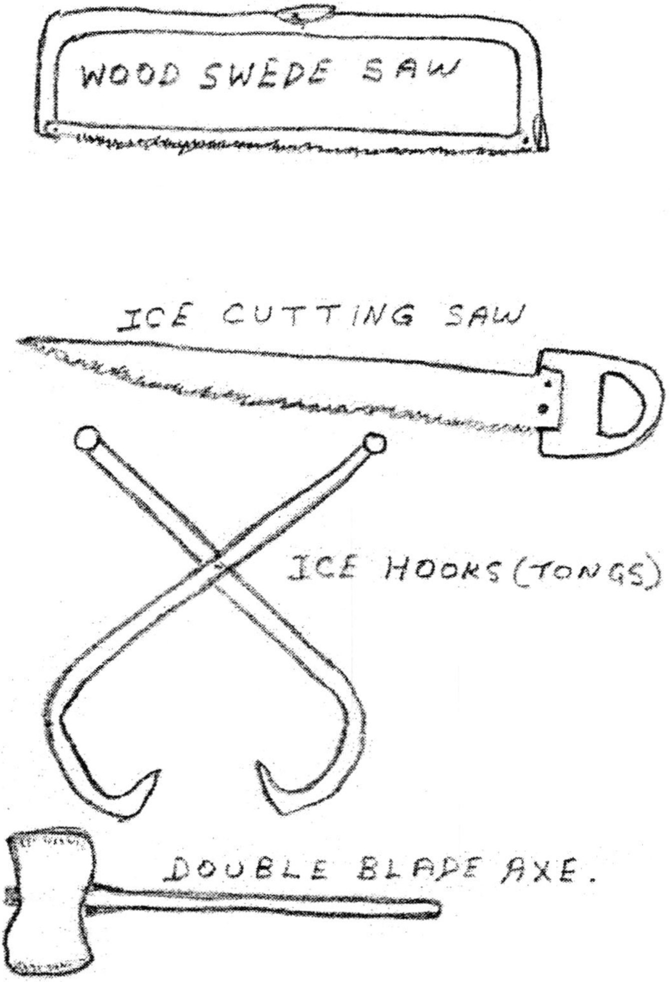

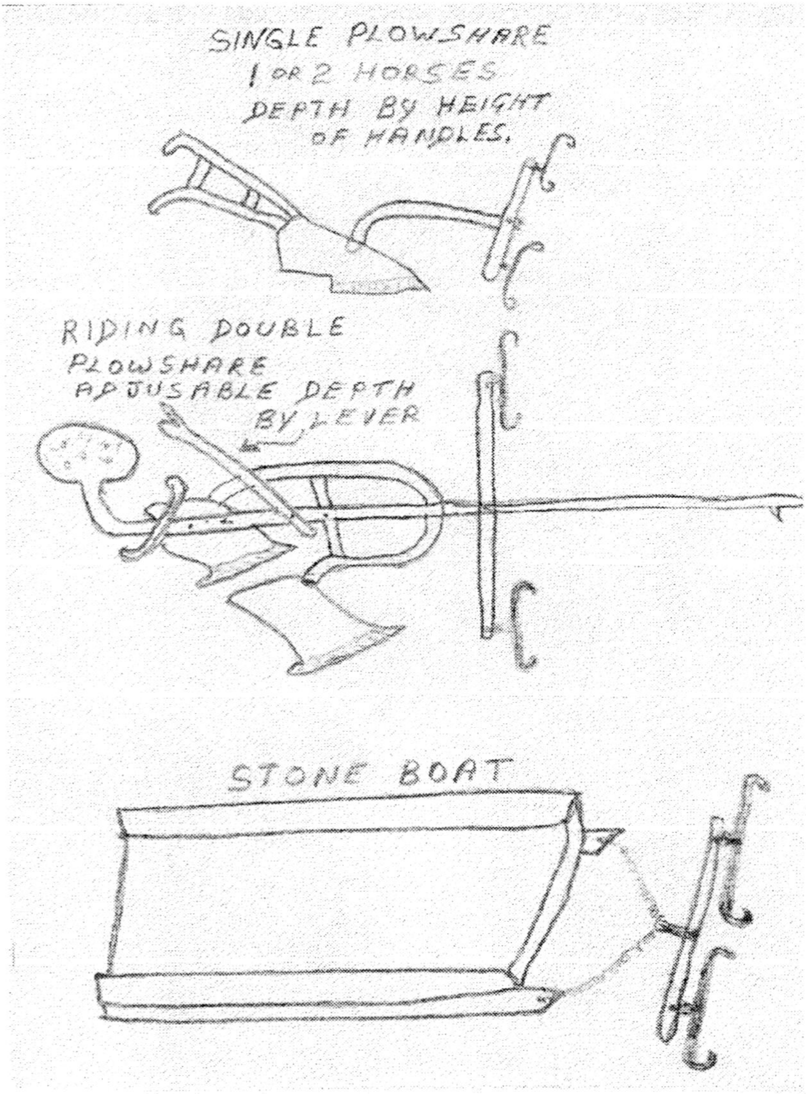
SINGLE PLOWSHARE
1 OR 2 HORSES
DEPTH BY HEIGHT
OF HANDLES.
RIDING DOUBLE
PLOWSHARE
ADJUSABLE DEPTH
BY LEVER
STONE BOAT

TWO HORSE
DIRT SLUSHER (SCOOP)

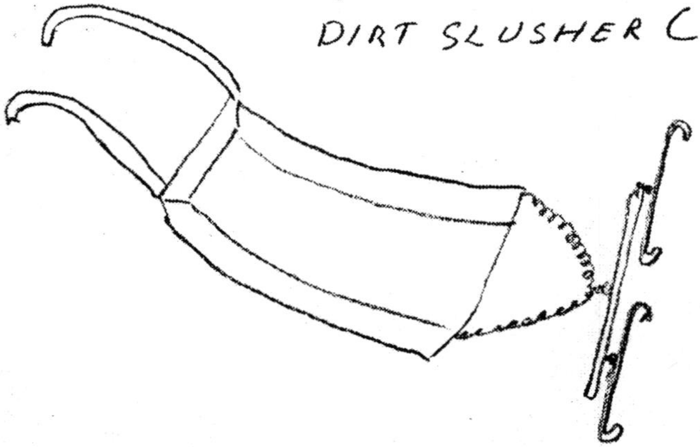

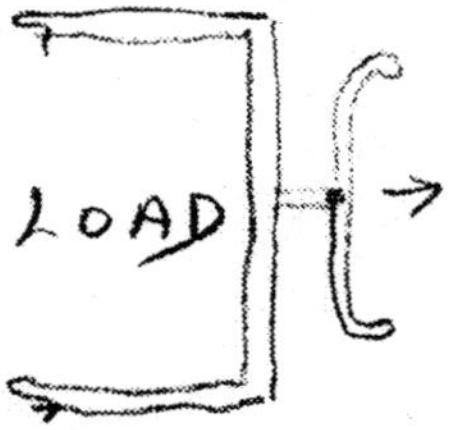

SINGLE TREE

TO ONE
HORSE HARNESS

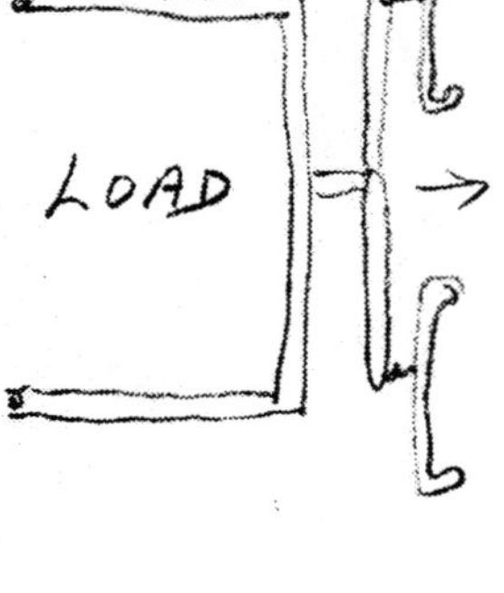

DOUBLE TREE

TO TWO HORSE
HARNESS

FREIGHT
CABOOSE
WITH STOVE
REIN HOLES
ONE OR
TWO
HORSES

TRAVEL
CABOOSE
WITH STOVE
ONE OR TWO
HORSES

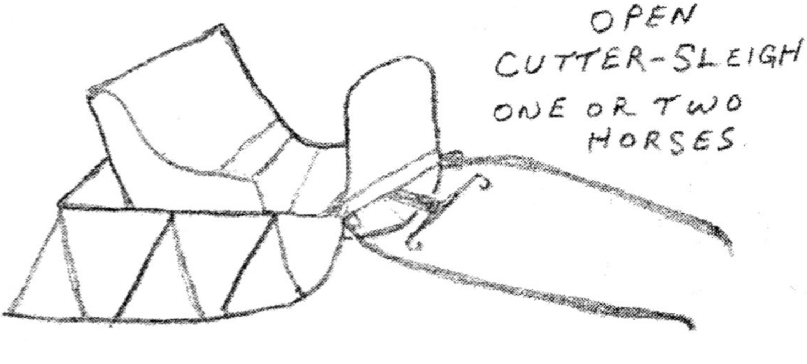
OPEN
CUTTER-SLEIGH
ONE OR TWO
HORSES.

HEATER

TWO 45 GAL. DRUM
STACKED HEATER

GRAIN ELEVATOR
POOL
OUT HOUSE
WELL PUMP
HAND WASHER
SHEAVE OF GRAIN
BINDER TWINE
STOOK OF SHEAVES.

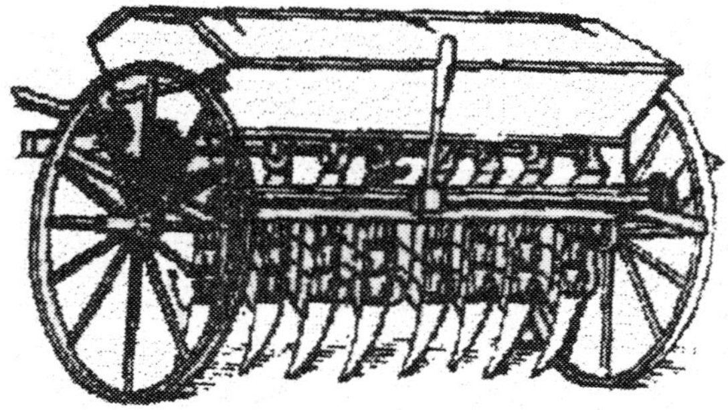

Seeder

Equipment Sales

1919 Case Tractor

Grain thresher

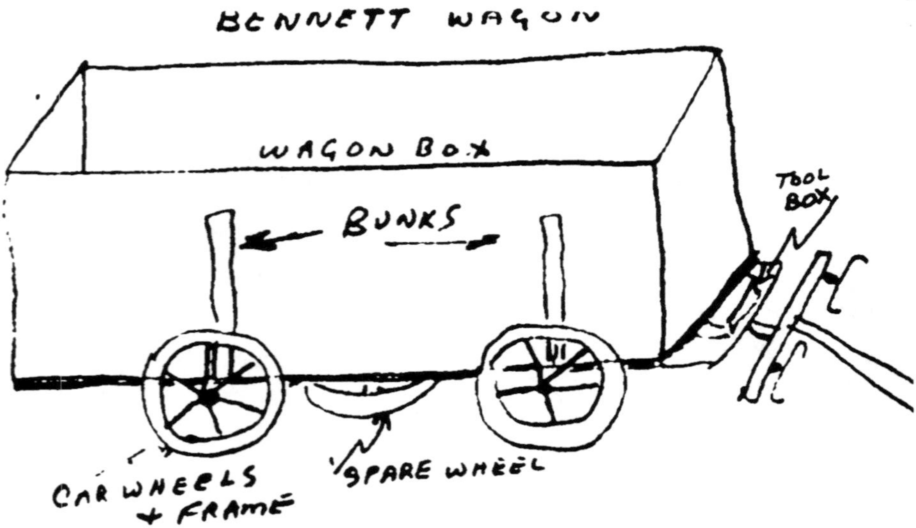

NOTE: JOHN'S BENNETT WAGON JUST HAD A FLAT BED. THAT WAY HE COULD USE THE WAGON BOX, OR SEATS AS A BUGGY. ALSO, THE FLAT BED COULD BE USED FOR HAULING LUMBER OR LOGS

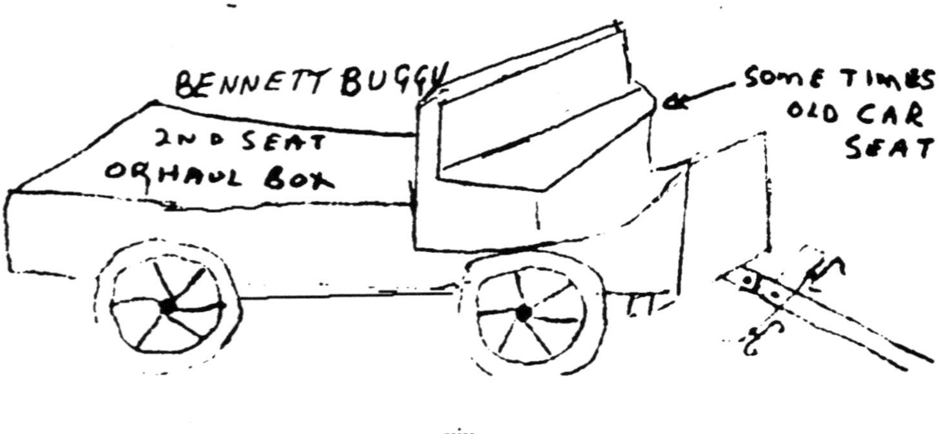

Contents

CHAPTER 1

A NEW WORK FORCE

It was near the end of November of 1931 when John heard about the Government giving farmers five dollars a month for every man they would give work and room and board. He and Florence talked about this and thought they would try and hire a few of these men who could find no work. The first thing they would have to do was make the bunkhouse bigger and put in tables and chairs for the men.

Florence said, "The cooking would be a lot of work but after the girls come home from school they could look after Ken. Helen was ten now and should be some help. That is if Flo didn't try to show her how everything should be done. Aileen at five could help keep an eye on him during the day. Maybe if you had Peter look after the men, cutting and hauling wood then you could look after the stock and be around here if you are needed. You could give Peter a few dollars more. He sure has earned it for the way he has worked for us."

"Yes", John replied, "He sure has done that. I will go into Pathlow and see Mr. Dahl at the municipal office and see what he can do for us. Then Peter and I better get going on the bunkhouse."

When John went to town to see Mr. Dahl he was told that he could arrange for some men early in the new year. There were some real good workers out there that just wanted three meals a day and a place to sleep. He also suggested that if John could afford it he would do real well if he gave the men the five dollars and a bit more each month. This would give them enough money to buy their tobacco and even go to the odd Saturday night dance. I know some real good men that would jump at a chance like that. How many do you think you can take on?"

"Gosh," John replied, "The bunk house will only sleep eight with Peter. The maximum I could handle would be seven. That will be a strain on my money but we will try it for a while and see how we make out. You can get word to me after the first of the year by some of my neighbours or if I don't hear from you by the end of the first week, I will come to town and see you."

"That sounds like a good plan.," Mr. Dahl answered. "I will get you some real good men."

"Thanks," John said, "I had better get home and finish that bunkhouse."

When John got home and had put the team away he went up to the house and told Florence and the kids that there could be up to seven more men living in the bunkhouse after the new year.

Florence stood there stunned for a while and then remarked, "God, I thought we were getting a few men, not a whole army. This will be like cooking for a threshing crew every day."

"I know," John answered. "We will all just have to pitch in and do whatever we can to help. With all the trees we cut, we should clear a lot of land and sell many loads of wood. We also can get lots of lumber cut and sell a few fence posts. I hear a lot of the farmers are wanting fence posts."

With this Helen butted in and said, "I can help with the cooking and look after the kids." Before Helen could say any more, Flo snapped back with, "I am not one of your kids. I can help just as much as you can."

Florence looked sharp at both Helen and Flo and said, "This is just the thing we don't need. If we are to help then we have to get along and not be fighting all the time. Is that quite clear to both of you?"

Both girls hung their heads and answered, "Yes mother, we won't fight any more. We will just help."

Aileen was standing behind the girls grinning her head off. John and Florence had a hard job to keep from laughing. They both knew that Helen and Flo had minds of their own and would soon have another spat.

John told Peter of their plans and that he would be getting more money if he looked after the men. Peter was real pleased with this and told John he would do a good job. John told him he was not worried about that -he knew he would do a good job.

The month of December was spent working on the bunkhouse. John and Peter added another room the same size as the one now. After they had added the three walls and put on the roof, they would put in the windows and then cut a big archway in the old wall. This way the one stove would keep both rooms warm. They would put eight bunks in the new room and leave the two bunks in the old room. They would put some furniture and shelves in the old room. That way the men could play cards and have a place to keep their belongings.

Florence was busy making up a mattress for each bunk. She was sewing used flour sacks together and stuffing them with soft straw. She was also making pillows and blankets but stuffing them with washed and dried chicken feathers. John had been killing and plucking a lot of chickens. Florence had been canning them to use later. They also put eggs up in "water-glass" to keep them for when they were short of eggs. The new men would eat a lot of eggs each morning. John had butchered his own pig and beef this year. They would need a lot of meat come January.

When John and Peter had finished the bunkhouse it was nearly Christmas time. They had not picked up the windows yet so had not cut out the arch in the old wall. Peter was sitting having a smoke and looking at their handy work. Peter turned to John and said, "You know John if I go to town and pick up the windows, maybe I could go over to my uncle's old farm and see if there is any furniture left behind. When he went back to Ontario he didn't take much with him."

"That's a good idea," John replied. "We can use whatever we can get. Tell your father that we will pay him something."

"I don't think they will want anything." Peter answered. "It is sitting there and not being used."

When Peter came back from town with the windows he had some furniture loaded on the sleigh. John came running over from the barn to see what he had. When he saw that there were two tables and three old dressers with drawers he was really pleased.

"What did this cost?" John asked. "You did real well."

"Not a thing," Peter replied. "Dad said he was glad to see someone get some use out of them. Anyway, his brother was happy to help someone who had been so good to his nephew."

"That's really nice," John said in a subdued voice. "We really appreciate what your family has done for us. I know the men will really be happy. Now they will have a place to store their stuff and a couple of good tables to play cards on. Seeing there already is one table in the bunkhouse, I may take one up to the house to add onto the one there. We will need a lot more space for eating soon."

"I thought you would," Peter said with a smile. "That is why I brought them both."

The windows were put in and the arch cut out between the two rooms. The dry logs that were removed would make good kindling for starting the fire in the stoves. Peter looked at the new bunkhouse and said. "I am sure glad you are getting some more men. It would seem awful big in here all by myself."

"Yes," John answered. "You might even get lost all by yourself. But when you get seven more bodies in here it won't seem so big."

Christmas was on a Friday in 1931, so Peter took off time from Christmas until the Sunday after New years. He said he would need to rest up for all the work John had planned for him starting in January. He also liked to spend the time with his family.

The Fords and Mullens spent Christmas and New years at each others place. The weather had been quite mild so the travelling back and forth was easy.

On New Year's Day the Fords were at the Mullens place. There was a lot of talk about John and Florence having seven more men working for them. Bart said he would buy some fence posts and would talk to his neighbours and see if they wanted any. He had most of his quarter section broken and wanted to fence it all in.

The only event that was a little scary that day was when Dora had gone upstairs to check on Ken and Ron to see if they were sleeping. When she went to come back down the stairs she stepped on a toy and slid all the way down the stairs on her behind. There was a window at the bottom of the stairs and one of her legs went right though the pane of glass. Everyone came running when they heard the thumping and could see what had happened. Dora looked fine and had not been cut by the glass.

"God," John shouted. "Are you okay. Dora?, Don't move we will - get your leg out of the window in a jiffy."

Dora still had her sense of humour and replied, "That would be a heck of an idea. I might just freeze my leg off if it is left out there too long!"

The men lifted Dora onto a chair and Bart was asking her if she hurt anywhere. Dora grinned and said, "My behind will be sore for a few days but other than that just my pride is hurt. I was lucky that my leg didn't get cut badly."

Everyone had a good laugh over this and were glad it had ended up the way it had. The children were warned about leaving toys on the stairs and all of them listened without saying a word.

John said there was a window in the bunkhouse the same size and they could take it out and board up the hole till a new glass could be brought from town. Bart and John went out to do this and on the way to the bunkhouse Bart said to John, "I think I need a trip to the barn for a drink of brandy. After that scare I need something to calm down my nerves."

"Hell of a idea," John said, "Dora sure brought the New Year in with a bang. But she scared the Hell out of us in the process."

Both men laughed and went into the barn to have another New Year's drink.

CHAPTER 2

AN EIGHT MAN CREW AT WORK

On the Sunday after New Year's when Peter came back from his time off with his family, he had some news for John. After he had put the horse in the barn he went up to the house to give John the news.

When Peter entered the house John and Florence both asked if he had enjoyed his time at home. Before he could answer, the three girls came charging out and started fighting to see who could hug Peter first. Peter just laughed and said, "Take it easy now, We don't want anyone trampled in the stampede. I will be here for a while so let's sit down on the sofa while I tell your folks some news I have for them."

The girls really liked Peter so they went into the living room to sit with him on the sofa. When everyone was settled Peter told John and Florence the news.

Well when I was in Pathlow last Thursday," Peter started, "I ran into Mr. Dahl and he asked me to tell you that your men will be in Pathlow on the two o'clock train next Friday. He suggested that you pick them up as they will have no place to stay the night. He said with your big caboose you should have no trouble bringing them to the farm. He also said they are good men and are willing to work hard. They come from all walks of life and have done many trades.

Some were cooks, blacksmiths, farmers and many other trades."

"Gosh," Florence said. "Maybe a couple of good cooks would be a great help around here. God knows I will sure need some."

John and Peter both laughed then John said, "We will see when the time comes. Maybe some will want to be inside out of the cold once in a while."

The girls were all excited about the new men coming to work at the place. This made Peter comment, "I guess you girls will have lots of attention now. You won't miss me as much when I go away."

The girls all said in unison, "No, no, Peter, you are still our best friend."

With this everyone had a good laugh. John and Peter talked of the things they would need for the workers. Florence had the bunks all ready with bedding. They had to pick up new glass for the window that had been broken New Year's Day. The bunkhouse seemed ready for use. They would have to get some more axes and Swede saws. A couple more log chains would also be needed. Florence said maybe they should pick up some leather mitts. She had already knit some gloves but with the cold weather, mitts would be needed. They sat and made up the list of things that Peter would go to town and pick up before Friday.

It looked like it was going to be a busy week ahead. There was much to be done in preparation for the coming of the new workers. There would now be fourteen mouths to feed instead of seven that were here now. The family will be doubled. Everyone agreed that they better get to bed early so they could have an early start in the morning.

Florence started early on Monday morning. She was putting an oil cloth cover on the new tables. This would make it easier to keep them clean. When John was finished making the two new benches she would cover them also.

John was making benches for the house and also a couple to put in the caboose so the men would have a place to sit on the way home. Peter was checking out all the equipment that they would need in the bush and listing what he would have to buy. He enjoyed his new job as foreman as John called him. It was a new challenge for him and he was looking forward to next week.

Peter went to town on Wednesday and picked up the supplies along with glass for the window. He also told Mr. Dahl that John would meet the two o'clock train on Friday.

On Friday John left at noon to meet the train. It took a good hour to get to town and he wanted to pick up a few things at the store. The weather was nice which made for a good trip to town.

Mr. Dahl met John at the train station and said he would introduce him to the men. He had not met them before but knew all their names. John thanked him and they went inside to wait for the train.

When the train came in from Regina there was a group of seven men who got off together. Mr. Dahl walked up to them and asked, "I guess you are the group that are going to work for John Mullen?"

"Yes," most of them answered. "We were told that he would be here to meet us."

"Yes, that is right." Mr Dahl replied. "My name is Dahl and I run the Municipal Office here. This is Mr. Mullen who prefers to be called John. He will be taking you to his farm. Don't try to introduce yourselves all at once. You can remember John's name but he will never remember all your names. You will have lots of time to get acquainted on the way to your new home."

Everyone nodded their heads then John said, "My caboose is that big one over by the barn. You can put your stuff in there if you want to. I will be leaving in about half an hour. If any of you want anything at the store, now is the time to get it. My farm is six miles from here and we only come in every week or so. I think you all know what your pay will be. Ten dollars a month with room and board. If any of you are a little short now, I will give you an advance so you can buy what you need.

Some of the men asked if they needed bedding, mitts and things like that.

John told them that all they would need is their own clothes and they should be good enough for outside work.

The men said they would take care of that and buy some tobacco and papers to last them a while.

John could see that the men were not moving so he said. "Let's go over to the store and you can give the owner your names and he will give you a five dollar credit and add it to my bill. That way you can get what you want with no trouble. I pay my bill every month so he won't mind at all."

The men all nodded and said they thought that was a great idea because some of them only had the clothes they had on and a few extra things in the small sacks they carried. They would be happy to have their own tobacco for a change and not have to bum smokes from everyone they could.

One of the men spoke up and said, "Hey, I think we are going to like this place of John Mullen's. He is already treating us like one of the family."

They all agreed and headed over to the store to buy what they needed.

By the time the men had bought their things at the store John had the team hooked up and a good fire in the little stove in the caboose. They all got in and found a seat. It was crowded but nice and warm. One of the men remarked, "This is travelling in real luxury. After riding the rods for the last few months it is nice to have a place that is warm and know we are going to have a place to sleep tonight. With a meal to boot." Everyone nodded or agreed with some remark.

John said that they would be about an hour or better getting to the farm. It would be a little slower with a bigger load for the team to pull. "This would be a good time to find out your names. If you want to add anything else, feel free. If you don't, no one will ask any questions."

The first man to speak up said, "My name is Joe. I was learning to be a blacksmith back in Ontario. When there was no work I just started riding the rods and picked up a little work here and there. Just enough to get the odd meal and sometimes a place to sleep. There are not many barns I have not slept in across Canada. I think everyone here has had about the same experience."

The next man to speak said his name was John but would go by the name Jack as there seemed to already be a John. Everyone laughed at this. He went on to say that he had been a carpenter back in Ontario.

The men went on to give their names and what they had done before.

Fred said he had been a baker back in Manitoba. Jim had been a farm hand in Saskatchewan, Cliff a ranch hand in Alberta, David a logger in British Columbia and George a miner in Nova Scotia.

When they had finished, John remarked, "Gosh, with all these different trades we will not have to look for any outside help on the farm. I must tell you though, that you will be mostly cutting trees and hauling them out of the bush."

David replied, "Hey, that doesn't sound too bad. The trees here are a lot smaller than in B.C."

"Well they might be a bit smaller," John. replied, "But there are a hell of a lot of them."

The men kept chattering and the next thing they knew they were at the farm. John stopped in front of the bunkhouse and they all piled out. John told them that they could go into the bunkhouse and pick their beds. He told them that they could wash-up in there and also they had their own outhouse behind the bunkhouse. He added that the barn was a lot warmer at this time of year. John also told them that now that it was four-thirty that supper would be in the house at five-thirty. He introduced them to Peter and said they could get to know each other in the next hour. Then at supper they could get to know his family.

Jim spoke up and said, "I think I would like to go to the barn with you and help with putting the team way. I have sort of missed being around stock."

"Great," John answered. "Anyone else who wants to look round, feel free. You won't be able to see much in the dark so don't wander off too far. We don't want to send out a search party looking for you."

This brought a good roar of laughter. John unhooked the team and left the caboose in front of the bunkhouse so the men could unload their things whenever they wanted.

When the men came in for supper John introduced them to his wife and kids. They all seemed pleased with the food that Florence had put out on the table. Everything was quiet while they enjoyed the good food.

Fred was the first one to speak up and he said, "Mrs. Mullen, that is the best meal we have had in months. We would all like to thank you."

Florence looked at Fred and replied. "Would you please all call me Florence? When you call me Mrs. Mullen, I think that my mother must be around someplace."

Everyone had a chuckle about this remark and it seemed to ease the tension in the room. The men were all young and a bit shy.

John then said, "Men tomorrow is Saturday and you can spend the day looking around the place. In fact, if you want to, you can do up your washing and have baths if you want to." He continued with, "That door there leads to a lean-to on the side of the house. The washing machine and tubs are in there. Also, there is a flat top wood stove for heating water. You can do your laundry in there and also have a bath. Sunday will also be a day off so some of you may want to use the room then. Monday, we will all get to work. So for the next couple of days just enjoy yourselves and do what you have to do."

Fred replied, "We will do that, John. And Florence, if you want any help with the cooking, I worked for a baker and would only be to glad too help you in any way. I know I can't cook as good as you can but maybe it will give me a chance to work in where it is warm."

Fred took a few good natured remarks about this then Florence said, "I would be grateful for the help you can give me. By the looks of what is left we may need two cooks around here."

Everyone had a good laugh and then headed out to the bunk-house.

CHAPTER 3

A BUSY START TO 1932

For the next two days the crew looked over the farm. They did up their washing, patched clothes and darned socks. They got to know each other, the Mullen family, and Peter.

Fred spent some time in the house helping Florence do the cooking. They got on real well if they could keep the kids from under foot. Fred baked up some pies and bread and kept the house smelling like a bakery.

Some of the other men split and carried in wood for both the house and the bunkhouse. They seemed to want to help in any way they could.

On the first morning when John was doing the chores, Jim and Cliff came into the barn and started talking to John.

Jim said, "John, I was a farm hand so how about letting me do some of the chores in the morning and at night, I could milk, feed stock or whatever you want?"

Before he could answer, Cliff spoke up with, "I was a ranch hand and know how to take care of stock and such so I can sure help also."

John thought for a minute then replied. "Sounds good to me, but I will check with Peter. He is the foreman and I don't want to step on his toes right off the bat. I am sure he will agree and I would be right pleased with the help."

Both men nodded and went up to the house for breakfast.

At the noon meal on Sunday, Peter told the men that they would get together in the bunk house after and go over the duties for everyone. He said that he and John had talked it over and had come up with some ideas and would also like some input from the men. They all nodded, finished their meal and went out to the bunkhouse.

When everyone had settled down, Peter started to go over their duties. "We will start with you, Joe. You are the blacksmith so your duties will be to keep all the equipment in good working order. You will repair all the harness, keep the log chains and sleighs in good safe working order. Also, you will keep all the axes and saws sharp."

"You are next Jack, being a carpenter, you can keep all the buildings in good repair. Also, any pens or fences that need repairing."

Now for Fred the baker. You will help Florence all you can. There are a lot of mouths here to feed so any help will be appreciated."

"Farm hand Jim, you are next. You will help John with the chores morning and night. He will lay out what you have to do."

"Cliff the cowboy. You will feed the stock and keep the hay and straw supply in good shape. This will include chopping the water trough free of ice."

"David the logger, you will be in charge of keeping the main house and bunkhouse in a good supply of wood. Also, it will be your job to keep all the stoves and chimneys clean so they will not catch on fire. Some of the wood we use has a lot of pitch and they need cleaning often."

"Last but not least, George the miner. We do not have any big holes to dig so we will find you a job. (Some chuckles followed this and George laughed the loudest). You will be our Jack of all trades. You will do the town runs when needed. John will call on you whenever he needs a extra hand."

"Now these are mostly extra chores and a lot of them will be done on Saturday. Some will be done every day. We will all cut and haul logs Monday to Friday. Saturday will be chore day and Sunday will be a day off." John said, If anyone wants to go to any Saturday night dances, a team and caboose will be free for you to use. Also on Sunday, if any one wants to go to church, there will be horses for them to ride or a caboose if there are more than one going. There is a United Church at Ethelton, an Anglican in Pathlow and a Catholic Church in St. Brieux. Weather will play a part in this as it can be rough sometimes. I think that is about all I have to say, so let's hear what you think."

The men were quiet for a while and then Cliff spoke up. "That sounds good to me. Looks like you and John thought this out real good. I don't know about George? he might go digging for coal in his spare time."

Everyone else nodded and agreed with what Cliff had said.

The next morning Peter got the men together and they hooked teams to sleighs and loaded them with logging chains, axes, saws, their lunch supplies and feed for the horses. It was a cold clear day but there was no wind. They headed across the yard and followed the road to the field then to the trees they would start cutting.

When they got to the place where they would cut Peter told them what they would do first. "We will start by clearing the snow from behind that patch of trees. We will leave those trees as a wind break. Some dry trees and limbs will be brought in and a good fire started. We will store our lunches by the fire so they won't freeze solid. Take those two buckets and fill them with snow. Hang them over the fire to melt the snow. When the water boils, add tea to one and coffee to the other. You have never smelled or tasted anything as good as this when it is cold."

Peter then said "This is the way we will start. If you want to change around after, that is up to you. Everyone, likes to get back to the fire once in a while to have a rest and a drink."

"We will start this way. George, you will be the driver. You will keep one team hitched to the sleigh. When you have a load then you will haul it to the farm yard. You will have three piles there. One for saw logs, one for fire wood and one for fence posts."

"Next, Jim and Cliff will take a horse each and with a single tree and log chains, snake the logs from the bush to the hauling sleigh. They will put them in three piles the same as in the yard."

"David, you will be there and cut them into lengths that can be put on the sleigh. You, Jim and Cliff will help George load the sleigh. Then he can take them back to the farm yard. He will be able to unload them by himself just by pulling out the bunk stake. But you be careful George, that you keep out of the way and don't get caught in the bite and covered with logs. John will be around so ask him to show you how to do it a couple of times."

"Fred, Jack and Joe, you will do the cutting. Drop the trees away from the snake trail so that the butt end of the tree is easy to hook on to with the log chain. All the branches and small trees are to be piled so they can be burned in the spring. Are there any questions?"

Fred was the first to speak.

"Yeah, do the snake guys get to ride the horse to and from the loading sleigh?"

"That's right Fred." Peter answered. "But remember you can change jobs with each other. I would like you to do this then you will be using different parts of your body and it will not be so hard on you."

Fred laughed and said, "That's good, I just didn't want to see those two cowboys getting all the soft work."

Everyone had a good laugh at this and started off to what they had to do.

Peter got a good fire going and hung the buckets to melt the snow for coffee and tea. He knew that men working out in this weather would soon need a good hot drink and something to eat.

The morning went fast and the men came to the fire for lunch at noon.

They all agreed that they had never been so hungry. Also, the coffee and tea smelled and tasted like nothing they had ever tasted before.

Peter laughed and said, "Remember this when you roll into bed tonight and every muscle feels like it is going to snap."

A few agreed and Joe said, "Yes, but we will have done a good day's work and had three good meals. When you ride the rods you are tired and hungry. Tonight we will just be tired."

Some of the men changed jobs with a little banter but most were happy just to be working and feel like they were doing something to earn their keep.

That night after the chores were done and the men were in the bunk house, John came in and said to the men, "Hey I hear you have done a good job today. By the looks of the three piles of logs in the yard I would say you have done very well. If anyone wants to come up to the house and pick up some cookies for your coffee afterwards you are welcome to do so."

There was silence for a while then Cliff the joker of the gang said, "If any of us has enough strength to make it that far we sure will take you up on the offer. I think it will be early to bed for most of us tonight. It has been a long time since we have done a good day's work but it sure feels good."

John thanked the men and left for the house.

CHAPTER 4

LOGGING, LUMBER AND WOOD

The land clearing went ahead most days. When it was real cold, windy or heavy snow was falling, other jobs were done. There was always some other work that could be done. Equipment had to be repaired and much of this could be done under cover or in the work shed. The men had put an old sheet iron stove in the work shed to try and keep it a little bit warmer. The heat didn't travel very far but at least you could warm your hands and keep the ever present coffee pot warm.

The three log piles were getting big. Joe had made up a wood cutting saw on a set of runners. It was not fancy but with the pieces he had picked up in St. Brieux, he had made up a shaft with a saw blade on one end and a belt- driven pulley at the other end. He had picked up parts from an old threshing machine. They had cost very little but now they could run a belt from the tractor to turn the saw blade and cut wood. With all the men on the farm they could cut wood any time they wanted.

The bad part about using the tractor was that it was hard to start in the cold weather. You had to heat the oil so that you could turn it over with the crank. Then it was a chore to get it going.

One morning they were setting up to do some wood cutting. They were setting the saw up by the wood logs. Some were heating the oil before starting the tractor. After the oil was heated and poured into the tractor, they tried to start it. After many tries it still would not start.

John shook his head and said. "I have an idea, Let's tie a rope around the flywheel with many wraps and hook up a team and let them spin the engine over. It will turn faster this way and maybe start."

Some agreed and some looked skeptical that this would work.

Joe laughed and said, "What the hell, it might just work. It sure beats trying to turn it over by hand!"

Jim and Cliff went to the barn to hook up the team. The rest got a heavy rope and turned it around the flywheel. They also tied the rope to a double tree to hook the team up to.

When they were finished, the team was there to be hooked up. John was on the tractor to adjust the spark and feed the throttle if it started.

Jim was driving the team and was ready to go. John nodded his head and Jim let out a whoop. The horses jumped into the harness and started away from the tractor.

The horses had pulled out about half the rope when the tractor let out a loud bang. The horses pulled harder. All of a sudden the tractor started and was winding the horses backwards toward the tractor. With the snow packed down they did not have good footing and could not stop from being pulled back.

David was leaning on an axe so he jumped forward and swung at the rope. On the third try the rope parted and the team flew ahead away from the tractor. The end of the rope was flying around the flywheel but the tractor was going.

John kept the tractor going until it warmed up then shut it down so the rope could be taken off the flywheel.

Most of the men were bent over in fits of laughter. David and Jim were sort of just standing with their mouths open and saying nothing. John jumped off the tractor and said,"God, that was different. Thank God logger David had the sense to cut the rope. But at least we got the tractor going and it will be easy to start now."

Cliff piped up with, "Thank goodness we have a logger on the crew. It only took him three tries to cut the rope."

Everyone was laughing now. No one had been hurt and the horses were fine.

David said, "Can you imagine what would have happened if the team had been pulled back into the tractor. All hell would have broken loose."

Joe countered with, "Yeah, if we have to do this again then we had better wrap the rope on the other way and still have David stand by with the axe."

This brought on another roar of laughter from everyone.

John then said, "Let's get the tractor going before it cools down. Tonight we will put the tractor in the workshop and let the stove keep it warm. I don't think we will want to try using the team again."

Everyone agreed and started setting up the tractor in front of the saw. They lined up the belt from the saw to the flywheel on the tractor. The saw seemed to run fine. Now they were ready to cut up some firewood. They had a lot to cut because there had to be enough for the house and bunkhouse next year. Also, John had sold a lot of wood to other farmers that had already cleared their land. He and George would have to start delivering as soon as the wood was cut.

The wood cutting saw that Joe had made up worked really well. He let the other men know that he was not only a blacksmith but a mechanic to boot. He was at the end of a few jokes but the men were really glad that he had done this as now they would be able to do the work instead of getting someone with a saw to come in.

January and February were a couple of busy months. Not only was there land clearing, log hauling and wood cutting, but there had to be ice cut and hauled to fill the ice house. A shed with a roof and open sides had to be built to store the lumber that would be cut in March and April. The firewood had to be delivered and a lot of the smaller trees were cut up into fence posts. These had to be delivered to the farmers that needed them. After paying the men, John would come out with a small profit.

Everyone was busy but they still had time for some fun. The odd Saturday night some of the men would go to Pathlow to the dance. If Sunday was nice, some even went to church. Some nights were spent in the house where the men played with the kids and played cards. Fred would make pull toffee and other good things to eat. Everyone enjoyed these nights, especially the kids. They were made a fuss over and they all liked these nights.

John had three teams now and they were kept busy every day hauling. Soon they would have to start hauling the saw logs to Mike's place to be cut into lumber. Mike would keep forty percent of the lumber and John would haul the rest home. He had plans to build a new house in the future so he wanted to store up as much lumber as he could. They would build the house on a hill about a quarter of a mile from the house they now lived in. This place would give them a nice view of part of the Carrot River Valley. From there you could see many farms, Ethelton and Melfort twenty five miles away. It would make a nice place for a frame house. Florence and John talked of this a few times.It was still in the future but a dream just the same.

As March came in the weather was not as cold. Logs were being hauled to Mike's for cutting and Spring was on its way. The men were starting to talk among themselves about what would happen in the Spring. Would they still have a job or would they be back riding the rods? They all hoped that they could stay on but they also knew John could not keep them on forever. They even suggested to themselves that they would work for five dollars less. They just wanted a place to be and get fed three times a day. Times were tough and the price of grain and other farm goods were dirt cheap. The Depression was hurting everyone.

One Sunday the men went to talk to John. They asked him what he had planned for the summer.

John thought for a minute and then said, "I have been thinking about that and maybe we can work something out so most, if not all of you, can stay on if you want to."

The men looked at each, other nodding their heads and grinning. They were waiting for what came next.

John continued, "I have a lot of land of my own to break. I will be breaking land for other farmers. There will be a lot of hay to cut as we have a fair amount of stock I can't do this all by myself. Maybe there will be some road work to do to fill in the rest of the time."

The men started to talk all at once, then Jack spoke up with, "We would all be pleased to stay on. We know times are tough and we are willing to take a cut in what you pay us now. We would be just happy to stay here and work. It has been like one big family to us. Just like home. If you can see your way clear we would all be very pleased."

Everyone agreed at once with these remarks. They were happy and liked working for Peter and John.

John said, "I will talk it over with Florence and let you know as soon as I can."

With this the men thanked him and went back to the bunk-house.

CHAPTER 5

SPRING AND SUMMER 1932

The months of March and April were mild and the snow started to go. There was much to do with the lumber shed to be built and the logs taken to Mike's to be sawed into lumber. Then John's share had to be hauled back and stored under cover for drying.

John and Florence had talked over keeping the men on over the summer. They decided they would. There was enough work to keep them going and if any of them could get work on the roads, they could have a team and make their wages that way.

Joe was checking over all the field equipment and the tractor so they would be ready for spring planting. Jack was building the lumber shed and any other repairs that needed done. Most of the other men were hauling logs, fence posts or wood. They wanted to get this done before the snow left. It was easier hauling by sleigh than with the wagon.

John had over sixty pigs now. Some would have to be taken to market. The price was still fair for good hogs. Some of the pigs would have to be castrated. This was not a pleasant job but someone had to do it. Cliff said he would do the job as he had done a lot of this on the ranches he had worked on. No one else wanted the job anyway, so John said he would help.

Some of the men were burning up the brush piles that had been piled up when they were cutting down the trees in the winter. John figured that if they could break up the land early then a late crop of oats could be planted and cut for winter feed for the stock.

The weather warmed and the earth started to thaw out. The first job was to haul away all the manure that had been put out behind the barn in a big pile. This was spread out on the field as it made good fertilizer when plowed under. This was hard work but better than doing it in the winter when it was frozen. The garden got a good thick cover of chicken manure as it was the best for growing plants.

There were eight cows now and seven young calves. There were a couple of year old heifers. The steers had either been butchered or sold.

One day when John was in Pathlow delivering some wood he ran into J.C. Reid. For some reason everyone called him J.C. They soon got around to talking about homesteading or farming as a lot of people were starting to call it now.

John said, "How is that farm of yours doing, J.C.? I hear you lost some cattle over the winter."

"Yeah John, that's right," J.C. answered. "I lost some up in the back pasture. When we went back to cut watering holes for them we found out there were some dead. We don't know if they died and then were eaten by the coyotes or if the coyotes killed them first then ate them. But I will tell you this in the next few days there were a hell of a lot fewer coyotes around. It took a while but we got most of them."

"Good," John replied. "I never did like those sneaky little buggers. They just aren't good for anything."

"Say, John," J.C. said, "I hear you have a few head now. Are you interested in selling or better yet trading some of them to me?"

John thought for a minute then replied, :"I don't know. What have you got to trade?"

J.C. grinned and said, "I must have something you could use.

As you know, I have a truck and a Baby Grand Chev car. I don't really need them both so how about a couple of heifers for the car?"

John shook his head and countered with "I only have two heifers so maybe you would go for a heifer and a couple of good brood sows? I have two that should kick out some little pigs in about a month."

J.C. thought for a minute then stuck out his hand to John. "You got a deal," he said. They shook hands and then started to talk over the finer parts of the deal.

John said that J.C. could pick out the heifer that he wanted and J.C. said he would deliver the car as soon as the roads were good enough to drive on.

John laughed and said, "Do you think the car will be able to get that far without breaking down?"

J.C. retorted with, "If you can keep your stock alive that long then the car will make it to your place."

Both men laughed and shook hands again. To a homesteader or farmer this was as good a way to keep a promise as anything drawn up by a lawyer.

When John got home that night he told Florence about the deal he had made with J.C. Reid.

Florence shook her head and said, "Just because you have a crew of men working for you and over a hundred acres ready for seeding it doesn't mean you have to drive around in a car like some tycoon from the big city!"

John grinned and said, "I thought it would be nice to use when we went to visit the Fords on Sundays and for quick trips to town. This would be easier on the horses and quicker. With the men working the horses six day a week it would give them a good rest on Sunday."

Florence stayed stern and said, "You have thought this out real good. If you shook hands on the deal then it is as good as done. And I don't think you would have if the deal wasn't done."

John had to admit that they had shook hands and the deal was done.

Florence softened up and said, "Now we own a tractor and a car. What will it be next?"

John replied, "I don't know but I will do some thinking about it."

Florence laughed and said, "I guess you will."

The weather got real warm and the spring planting was in progress. The cleared land was ready to break as the brush piles had all been burned. The stumps were pulled while the soil was soft and it looked like they may be able to plant a crop of oats for winter feed. The wild strawberries were starting to show up as the spring had been so early and mild.

One day Florence decided to go picking strawberries so she packed up the kids and put Ken in the buggy with a few pails and started off to pick strawberries.

They would cut across the farm on a logging road that led to where the new house would be built some day. When they got to the main road they would go down the big hill then up to the grass land that would have some strawberries. Helen and Flo were taking turns pushing the buggy and Aileen was coming behind with a couple more pails. Helen and Flo were yapping about they were getting longer times at pushing the buggy. Florence had about enough so she turned to the girls and said, "If you two can't get along then I will put you in the buggy and let Ken push you. You are acting like a couple of spoiled brats. I brought you along to help, not fight all the time."

With this the girls shut up and pushed the buggy but not without a few dirty looks at each other.

When they had got about half way down the big hill, Aileen said, "Mom, look at the big dog and pup at the bottom of the hill."

Florence looked down the hill and froze in her tracks. It was not a big dog but a mother bear and her cub. She turned around and said in a low stern voice, "You all turn around now and very quietly start back for home."

Florence stood for a minute and watched the bear. She did not seem to pay much attention to them so she turned and followed the girls.

Sometime after they had got home Florence started to breathe normally. It had been a scare but everything was all right now.

That night when everyone was sitting around the table it was quiet. John spoke up and said, "Everything seems to be going good this spring. What did you do today, Florence?"

"Oh we went to pick strawberries but there was a bit of a setback so we didn't get to pick any."

"What kind of a setback ?" John asked.

"Oh, we had a bear and her cub on the road so we decided to come back home for today."

"Jesus," John exclaimed. "You mean a real bear?"

"Yeah, a real bear. Aileen thought it was a big dog with it's pup. I just wish it had of been. I don't want to go through that again."

Before John could say any more, Fred spoke up and said, "You will not go picking strawberries alone any more. All of us will go out on Sunday and pick all the strawberries you will need. I think it was just a stray bear being as spring was so early but we can't take any chances. What do you say men?"

All the men nodded their heads and agreed with Fred.

John echoed their thoughts. "That sounds like a good plan to me. Maybe later on it will be safe for you to go out berry picking. Let's wait until the raspberries are ready and we will look at it then."

John went to Pathlow and came home with another surprise in early June. He brought home a radio. It was a Columbia and ran on batteries. It would pick up many stations with the wire aerial he had run out to a big tree top.

Florence wasn't too pleased but she was used to these kind of little surprises. What would be next she would never know.

On June the twenty-first the house was full of people. They had come to hear the big fight between Jack Sharkey and Max Schmeling. It could be picked up from many stations in the United States. Everyone sat in front of the radio and listened to every word that was said. A few bets were made on the fight. The fight went for fifteen rounds and Jack Sharkey won. Some were happy and some that lost bets were not. John was heard to say, "I'm glad the German lost." This went back to his service in the First World War.

Everyone enjoyed coffee and sweets afterwards. They all thanked John and Florence and went home happy.

The rest of the summer went well. John used the old Chev. to go back and forth to where he was breaking land for other farmers and everyone worked hard. The hay crop was good but without much rain it looked like the crop would not be as good. They would just have to wait till Fall and see what happened.

CHAPTER 6

FALL 1932

With the early warm Spring the snow had left fast. The rest of the Spring and Summer had been dry and hot. The grain had started good, but by mid-July the soil was dry and the crop was starting to mature early. This would make for an early harvest and poor yield. There had been a lot of thunder storms but little rain fell. The oat crop on the new broken land did real well and a good yield of winter hay feed was taken off. The hay back in the hills by the sloughs had come fast and had to be cut early. The garden did well as the men hauled water on Sundays and kept the vegetables in good shape.

Florence and the men had got a lot of strawberries and raspberries before it got too dry. The saskatoon and choke cherries dried up fast and there would not be a lot of jam and jelly from them. The cranberries looked like they would not be too good come fall.

By mid-August the barley was ready to harvest and the wheat would not be far behind. The grain was short and not good big heads like there should be from a crop.

Some of the men went to work on threshing crews. They had built two more hay racks so they used John's horses and were able to get an extra dollar a day. The harvest was over fast as the weather stayed hot and dry so no time was lost to wet conditions.

Aileen started school this Fall so that only left Ken at home. Florence missed Aileen because she had kept an eye on Ken most of the time. Now Florence would be by herself and this took up a bit more of her time. With the three girls away all day it sure was quiet around the house.

It stayed so dry and warm that John was able to get all the fields turned over before the cold weather came. Some years you had to wait for Spring before you could plow your fields.

Peter was working with the men to get things ready for the winter work. It seemed odd to be working on sleighs and winter equipment when it was still warm and dry.

John and George were hauling the wheat to the grain elevators. Some of the grain was getting not much more than a few cents a bushel. John had decided to raise more pigs so he sold his wheat and bought barley at a cheaper price.

The price of hogs was still good so John took about sixty to be sold. He wondered why the price was still up but he guessed someone still had money and liked their bacon and eggs. He hoped it would stay that way because he was going to raise more now.

Everyone thought with the hot dry summer that the winter would be long and cold. They were not disappointed. Just past the middle of October it started to snow real hard and the temperature dropped well below zero. The men were rushing to get the stock in from the pastures and close to feed. Some of the roads to the pastures were filled with snow drifts and had to be broken out on horse back. Some of the drifts were so hard that the horses could walk on top of the snow. This was not good as sometimes they would go through and could not move their legs, then they had to be dug out with a shovel. By the time the road was broken through the stock had to be hurried back to the corral before it drifted in again. John was happy that he had extra help because he could never have done it alone and would have lost some of his stock.

The barns and pens were warm and the men had piled straw around the chicken pens to help keep in the warmth. The extra horses and cattle that could not be fit into the barn were kept in the corral behind the barn. They had also piled straw up along the pole fence to help break the wind. It was not only snowing hard and cold but the wind seemed to be blowing all the time. If this was any indication it would be one hell of a long cold winter.

Clearing land was far from everyone's mind. It kept everyone busy just keeping up with the stock, putting wood in the house and bunkhouse. The water trough had to be chopped out twice a day to water the stock. The pump had to be primed with hot water to get it started. The stove in the shop was kept going all day so there was hot water ready at all times. Even the pigs grain was mixed with hot water so it would not freeze before they could get it eaten.

The car and tractor had to be dug out and covered. The snow had come so early that it had caught everyone by surprise and a lot of the Fall chores had not been done yet. The car would stay there until Spring and the tractor would be moved into the work shed when the weather got mild again.

The temperature stayed well below freezing for a good month. Only two trips had been made to town and that was to pick up the mail and a few supplies. John and George had made these trips in the small caboose and it had upset once when they went over a slanting snow drift. This caused a bit of excitement but they were glad they had both gone along. Being as they had the small caboose they could push it up back on the sleigh. The little stove had spilled hot coals and burning wood inside. They had to hurry to get them back into the stove before it started a good fire and they lost the caboose.

Everyone was glad when a trip was made to town because then there were newspapers to read and a fresh supply of tobacco.

At night everyone sat around the radio and found out that the rest of the country was not much better off than they were. Without the radio they would have been long boring nights.

When the weather got mild toward the end of November the

men started to cut trees in the bush. The snow was deep but not hard in the trees. Once a road had been broken through and packed down it was not too bad working in the bush.

One day at supper time John said to no one in particular, "You know, it was so cold that I missed the November the eleventh get together at the Legion and if the weather stays like this all winter we will bloody well miss Christmas and New Year's with the Fords."

Florence gave John a scowl and said, "You know John, the weather is just about as bad as your language."

Before she could say more there was a roar of laughter from everyone but John.

"I'm sure glad that I am able to make everyone happy again," John snapped. "The spirit around here is about as low as a sow's belly in the snow."

Everyone roared at this even, John.

The weather stayed cold but clear most of the time. Beef and pigs were butchered and hung in the meat shed. With this kind of weather the meat would never spoil. The tough part was sawing it up into smaller pieces after it had been hanging for a while. A lot of roosters were killed and Florence bottled them for future use. The vegetables had been stored in the root cellar below the house and covered with sand. They would keep there without freezing in the cold winter.

At the end of December a Chinook from the west moved in and in six hours the temperature went from forty below to forty above. This was like going from winter to summer in a very short time. If it stayed for a while and it went cold again, the snow would freeze like ice and travelling would be very tough going.

It stayed mild until the end of the first week in January. The Mullens and the Fords were able to go back and forth for the holidays. Peter went home over vacation. The rest of the men went to Melfort to have a good time. Cliff and Jim stayed home and looked after the stock for John. They were treated like family and joined in with everyone else when the Fords came to the Mullens.

After a nice Christmas holiday the men came back ready to work at some more land clearing. They all hoped that the worst of the winter was over. But only time would tell.

CHAPTER 7

1933 START OF HARD TIMES

By the middle of January, the weather had turned cold again and the snow was hard enough to walk on the top. This made it a little tougher to work in the woods. The breaking of new trails to haul the logs out was hard work. The men worked hard and had good piles of logs for sawing wood, lumber and fence posts.

The Depression was starting to catch up with the farmers. The price of grain was low and the crops had not been that good. John made more out of selling wood and pigs.

One night after the kids had gone to bed John and Florence were talking about what they would have to do to get by.

John said to Florence, "You know we can't keep the men much longer. There is just not enough to pay them all."

Florence nodded her head and replied, "For the price we are getting for grain it doesn't pay to clear more land for farming. If it wasn't for the wood and lumber, it would be really bad."

"Yeah," John agreed. "We have a good pile of lumber for our new house but can we afford to build with the extra costs? We sure will have to think of something if we ever want to build that house."

They both would have to come up with some way to make things easier to keep above board. They did not want to end up broke. Thank goodness the payments were low and John had the pension cheque coming in every month.

A couple of weeks later John was in Pathlow and was talking to Mr. Dahl (everyone called him Mr.) at the municipal office. They were talking about the bad times and how some people were thinking of giving up their farms as they could not make ends meet.

John told Mr. Dahl that he was going to have to let his men go as he just could not afford them any more. He did not want to do this but he could not see what else to do.

Mr. Dahl nodded and said. "Those men you have are real good workers from what you have told me. Maybe we can do something to help you and them out. I have been asked to get six good workers to go to Flin Flon to work in the mine. They would be needed for the first week in May."

John looked at Mr. Dahl and replied, "That would be just great. I have not wanted to let these men go as they are just like family. The kids and us have really got attached to them. But if you have a job for them, that would make it easier for everyone."

Mr. Dahl said he would make the arrangements and John could let him know who the six would be.

John thanked him very much and went away feeling much better. He would have to talk this over with Florence.

When John got home that night he and Florence talked over what they would do as there were eight men and the mine only wanted six. John said he would talk to the men tomorrow and work something out with them. Florence said she would talk to the kids as they would not be happy with the men going as they had been spoiled by them so much.

John agreed then said, "Let's try and keep Jack on if he wants to stay. He is a good carpenter and if we can start on our new house he would be the one to do it. I can drive nails if someone tells me where. We have a good supply of lumber so maybe we could make a start in the summer.

Florence agreed so they left it at that.

The next morning after breakfast John told the men he would like to meet with them in the bunkhouse. They looked at each other but said nothing, but they all expected the worst.

When they had all settled down in the bunkhouse John heaved a big sigh and said, "As you all know, I can't keep you all working much longer".

The men looked at each other and shook their heads. They had been expecting this day for a long time. It just seemed so hard when it finally came.

John kept talking. "It is not all bad news. There are six jobs in the mine at Flin Flon starting the first week of May. This would take care of all but two of you."

Before John could say more, Peter spoke up and said,. "I would not be able to go to Flin Flon as my dad is not doing too well and needs help with his farm. I have been wanting to tell you for a long time but thought I would be letting you down. So now you are down to one extra."

John spoke up quickly, "I would like Jack to stay on as we hope to build a new house with the lumber we have cut. It is going to take a couple of years as winter work is out of the question so if you will stay, Jack, I would be really pleased."

Jack did not hesitate in his answer. "John you know this has been my home for a while and you have treated us just like family. I would be most happy to stay on and maybe in a couple of years things will get better and we will all have jobs."

All the men clapped their hands and yelled their approval. Then Cliff spoke up and said, "John, we are all sorry to have to leave here by May but we know the problems you are having to make ends meet. You have done a great job of finding us some place to go but we are afraid you will work our asses off in the next couple of months."

This broke the tension and everyone had a good laugh over

Cliff's remarks. John just left the bunkhouse with a big lump in his throat.

For the next couple of months the men worked extra hard. They hauled logs for lumber. Cut a big pile of fire wood and cut and delivered some fence post. There would not be as much wood needed now but it would not spoil.

Before the end of April, plans were made to have a big dinner for the men. It was decided that Sunday, April the 23rd would be the day. This would give the men a chance to clean things up and get to Flin Flon by Monday the 1st of May. The Ford family would be invited as they knew the men well and would enjoy the get together .

With Spring on the way, Joe looked over all the machinery to get them ready for spring planting. With just John and Jack they would not want anything to break down as they would be busy enough without any trouble.

Sunday, the 23rd of April came and it was a real nice sunny day. The men were busy putting up extra tables and chairs for the dinner. Fred was working in the kitchen helping Florence and the kids were getting in the way all over the place. There was a lot of joking and laughing going on. Everyone wanted to make this a real nice day.

The Fords got there about eleven for the first meal at noon. This would be a roast beef dinner. There would be a turkey cooked for supper. As usual there would be no shortage of food.

The afternoon was so nice that the men were able to go outside and have a few games of horseshoes. There was much laughter and fun, probably helped by the odd trip to the barn to have a sip of brandy or whiskey. Florence and Dora didn't mind as it left them some time to talk.

After supper everyone was sitting around reminiscing about the times they had spent together.

Later in the evening, Peter went out to the bunkhouse and came back with a box. He asked everyone to listen as he had something to say.

He started with. "The men and I have really enjoyed working here. We were taken in when there was nothing to do and very little to eat. Some nights we never even had a good place to sleep. We have decided to show our appreciation to John and Florence for putting up with us for the past while. So I will ask Jim to do the honours for John. They worked together the most."

Jim reached into the big box and lifted out a package. He then said. "John we are sorry to be leaving but we must all do what has to be done. This is a little gift to show you how much we appreciate what you did for us here on the farm."

Jim handed the gift to John and asked him to open it. John started to open the gift.

When he had it open, there was a bottle of brandy and a cigarette holder.

John looked at them for a minute then in a husky voice said, "Thank you very much. This brandy will give more reasons to spend lots of time in the barn and you all know how I hate it when the cigarette paper sticks to my lips. Thanks again."

Everyone clapped and then Fred got up and picked out a package from the box. He then said, "Florence, you and I have worked together in the kitchen many times. So we thought you could use something to help you there." He handed Florence the package.

Florence opened the package and then with some composure, said. "Thank you for the brooch to hold my hair back when I am cooking. Fred often had laughed at me putting a dish towel around my head to keep my hair out of the food. Also, thank you for the subsciption to the women's magazine. I am sure I will enjoy many hours reading."

John was heard to say, "I will need a shot of that brandy if I have to say anything more."

Everyone who heard thought this was funny and enjoyed themselves for the rest of the evening.

CHAPTER 8

SMALL SCALE FARMING

The Spring of 1933 would be some different as now there was only Jack to work with John. The snow was gone early so Spring planting began. The garden had to be put in and some more pigs were ready for market.

The crop planting went well and by the first of June everything was in and now it was up to the weather to do it's job.

John and Jack started to break some land. There was only about seven acres cleared that could be broken. There were a lot of rocks in this area so it made the work slow.

One twenty acre plot in the north-west corner of the farm was just small shrubs and a few trees mostly along the creek. John just drove the tractor over the small trees to loosen up the soil. Then he spread some Timothy and Clover seed by hand. When this started to grow it would be a pasture for the stock. A fence was put around the area to include the creek. There would be water there until the middle of July. Another fence was put in close to the property line fence and ran back up to the area behind the barns. This way the stock could come up for water when the creek went dry.

The strawberries came good this year and the raspberries looked good. Florence and the kids were kept busy picking for canning. Jack and John would help on Sundays.

Haying time came and a good many loads were hauled and stacked behind the barns. The weather was dry and hot now and rain was needed to help the crops grow.

Around the first of August, John and Florence decided that they might as well make a start on the new house. They marked out the spot on the top of the hill on the west side of the property. It would be about a quarter of a mile from the South property line.

When Florence and John were marking out the spot the kids were all over the place. They expected the house would be done in a week or so. After Florence explained to them it would be a year or so that slowed them down for a while.

Florence, John and Jack were talking over how they would build the house.

Florence asked Jack if he could draw up a plan for them.

"Sure," Jack replied. "You just give me a idea of what you want and I can sketch out a plan."

"Good," Florence answered. "I want a big kitchen, a dining room, a good-sized living room and one bedroom downstairs. The upstairs you can figure out."

John then exclaimed , "God, we will have a mansion. Do you think there is enough lumber to build a house that big?"

"Oh, I think so," Jack replied. "The biggest cost will be all the nails you will have to buy."

They all had a good laugh at this remark.

John said he would like a full-sized basement. One that was good and deep so they could store a lot of wood and have one corner with a big sand bin to keep the root crops from freezing. With the sand pit that was on the property, they would have a good supply. They would also be able to use the sand with the gravel to make cement for the walls. John would have to haul the cement and gravel from Pathlow. The first thing they would have to do is scoop out the hole for the basement. When the weather was not right for field work, he and Jack could work on the basement.

Jack came up with a good idea. He suggested that now that the bunkhouse would be too big, that he live in the front part and the other part be used as a shop. It would be warm in the winter and he could start making up window and door frames. This would save a lot of money not having to buy them.

Everyone agreed that this was a good idea. Now they had better get working on the plans.

Florence stopped and looked out over the landscape and said. "It is so pretty up here on the hill. I think we will call this place "Hill Crest Farm," you can see a good portion of the Carrot River Valley from here. Look at Melfort over there and it is twenty five miles away."

John said to no one in particular, "God, we haven't started yet and she already has the placed named."

"Well, John." Florence snapped, "If we are going to do all this work we may as well call it something nice."

"OK, OK." John said with a grin, "If it makes you happy, we will call the farm Hill Crest. I was only kidding anyway."

With this everyone headed back to the house with many things on their mind. There was much planning to do and a lot of work ahead for them.

August brought on rain and it looked like there was going to be too much for the crops. John and Jack took advantage of this wet weather and started work on the new house. They took the slusher and a team of horses and started to scoop out the basement. They would take the dirt down the hill and build up the slope in front of the house. The house would face east away from the main road. The dirt in front would make it level so a road could be put in a U around the house and back to the main road. One part would carry on down to the trees where the farm buildings would be built. They would be a little distance from the house but would be in the trees and part out of sight. The land was clear in front of the house and on both sides. Between the house and the road would be a nice spot to plant some grass. The cleared land on both sides would make a good gardening place.

The men got the basement dug and ready for putting in forms. Jack would work at this while John hauled the gravel, sand and cement. They worked on this until they were able to harvest the grain.

The harvest was not great this year but by selling the better grain and buying poor grain the stock would be well fed. The price of grain was low so, it was better to raise hogs and beef. They now had a quite a few hens and roosters which would help keep them going.

After the harvest the weather stayed nice. John and Jack decided that they would try and pour the cement before the cold weather started. They got Bart Ford and a couple of other neighbours to help them. The forms were twelve feet high. Ten feet below ground and two feet above.

When Bart arrived to help he said to John, "Jesus, John you have this basement halfway to China. You could have got Chinamen to help as they are probably closer than us."

Everyone had a good laugh at this and started work. It was going to take a day or two to get the job done. All the water had to be hauled in and the cement mixed in a big shallow box.

Florence was busy feeding the men and bringing them a snack mid-morning and mid-afternoon. The men drank gallons of tea and ate piles of sandwiches.

The job took most of four days to complete. By the time the men finished they were tired and had aches they had never had before.

When they were finished, John told Bart that when he went to Ethelton he would drop off a few loads of fence posts. He also told the other men that were there to help themselves to firewood from the big pile behind the bunkhouse. He said that they had cut up more than he needed and to be sure they took enough.

The men said that it wasn't necessary to do this but John insisted that they do so. He said that they would have never got the job done without their help. Now the basement was ready to be build onto in the Spring.

Now ahead of everyone was the job of getting ready for another winter. Everyone was wishing for a more mild winter than last year.

John had not used the car over the summer and it was just another expense that was not needed. He had not bought batteries for the radio but would do so for over the winter. The nights were too long not to have something to do besides read. The kids liked the radio and Florence liked to listen to daytime plays and opera music while working around the house.

Now it was time to kill roosters, beef and hogs. It was time to get the winter supply of meat in. Florence would be doing a lot of canning and everyone would be busy for the next while.

CHAPTER 9

WINTER 1933-34 AND HOUSE BUILDING

The first part of the winter was not too bad. John and Bart had got to the November eleventh day at the Legion. The wives had a good visit and the kids had a good time together.

When the weather was not too cold, John and Jack would cut trees. They were clearing for the new barn and pens that would be needed at the new house. Most of the trees were not too big so they were either hauled for fire wood or left to be squared off to make the new barn with. They were able to leave the poles there for when they were needed. On the cold days Jack would work in the shop making window and door frames. John would spend his time in the other shop repairing harness and other things that needed repaired.

Florence only had Ken at home so she could spend her time about the house as there was a lot to be done. She still had seven mouths to feed and she did all the sewing and knitting of any heavy outside wear.

John made at least one trip a week to town. He would pick up supplies and also pick up whatever Alex Mann next door needed. In the winter time it was hard for Alex to make these trips so John would do whatever was needed. This usually resulted in a few beers and some more western books to read. Alex was a good neighbour and never asked for much. But even though his war injury kept him mostly at home, he was always willing to help in any way he could. John and Florence felt sorry for him living alone. She would send fresh baked bread over with John whenever he went to see Alex. Sometimes she would send over a jar or two of jam. Alex read a lot and would send over all of his magazines. It was a good relationship and the type of thing that happened between farmers.

Christmas was on a Monday this year so it made for a good holiday. The Mullens and Fords went back and forth for the holidays. The weather was nice so Jack decided to take some time off and went by train to Saskatoon for ten days. Everyone agreed that the break from the farm would do him good. John had made arrangements to pick him up on January the 2nd at the five o'clock train in Ethelton.

With the festive season behind them, it was time to get back to the work of running a farm.

January and February were cold months. Some days John or Jack would hook up to the caboose and give the kids a ride to school. It was only abut three-quarters of a mile but one could get very cold even in that distance. School got out at three as it was dark by three-thirty. Being three hundred miles north of the forty-ninth parallel the daylight hours in the winter were quite short. All the chores with the stock were done in the dark. One had to keep a good supply of coal oil for the lanterns.

When March rolled around, the weather started to warm up. There had not been a lot of snow this winter so John decided to haul what logs he had to be sawed up into lumber. He and Jack had to help with the firewood cutting this year so that took up a couple of weeks time. It was a change for Florence to have a few men to cook for when they cut wood at their place.

One night when the three adults were sitting in the living room and reading, Jack spoke up and said, " You know John, when I have been in Pathlow getting lumber for the window frame and doors, I talked with a man who is also a good carpenter. His name is Ken Doolittle. You know, if you could see your way clear, it might be a good idea to have him work on the house and then I could help you when needed. It's your money. I am just making a suggestion."

John looked at Florence then said, "We will sure have to think about that. It sounds like a good idea as the house could be ready by late Fall. Thanks Jack I will look into the matter. One thing-I don't think we can stand two Kens around here. One is about all we can handle."

Just before they went to bed that night, Florence and John talked about getting Ken to work on the new house. They thought that it was a good idea so John would go see him the next time he went to Pathlow

A few days later when John went to Pathlow for some supplies he would look up Ken Doolittle. When he was at the lumber yard picking up some things for Jack he asked the owner if he knew where he could find Ken.

The owner pointed over to a man who was looking over some lumber. He said, "That is Ken over there. He is picking out some lumber for a small repair job that he is doing.."

John thanked him and went over to talk to Ken.

When John got to Ken he stuck out his hand and said, "I am John Mullen and I am told that you are a good carpenter."

Ken shook hands with John and said. "I am Ken Doolittle as you must know and I like to think that I am a good carpenter."

John replied with, "I would like to talk to you about coming to my place and helping to build our new house. What do you say we go over to the cafe and talk about it over coffee and pie?"

"Sounds like a good idea to me," Ken said. So they headed over to the cafe.

Over the pie and coffee they talked about the new house. They made a deal on the wages and Ken would start on the first of June.

He knew that Jack would work with him some of the time and was glad he would have help with some of the heavier work that would require two workers. He also knew he could stay in the bunkhouse with Jack on days he did not want to travel the six miles home. He thought this was a good idea as some nights the weather may not be good and after a long days work it would be nice to not have to travel home every night.

"Seems like we have a deal then," John said. They shook hands again and said that they would see each other again on the first of June.

The snow went fast and the farmers were able to get to work in the fields early. It looked like it would be another dry year. Without some rain and the early melt of the snow, crops would have a hard time growing.

The far pasture was coming up good and green. The extra stock except for the milk cows were kept down there. The creek would have water for awhile. If the weather stayed this dry then the gate would have to be opened to let the stock come up to the well for water.

On the first of June Ken showed up for work. He was shown the bunkhouse and shop. Then they went over to the new house and looked it over. Jack came along to help explain to Ken what they had planned. He had his sketch along and went over it with him.

After this was done Ken said, "This looks like a good plan and will be easy to follow. I will stay the odd night in the bunkhouse as I may work late if the weather is good. Also, I hear what a good cook Mrs. Mullen is and would like to get in on some of her cooking."

John laughed at this and said, "You had better call her Florence or she will figure that you think she is old."

They all had a laugh and then headed back to the shop where Ken had left his tools.

The hay season was early and not a great crop. Even the berries this year seemed to be smaller and dried up fast. The garden was coming good as it got watered once a week. It was important that one had a good garden to help get through the winter.

Once the hay crop was cut and stacked behind the barn, Jack started helping Ken on the new house. John worked on squaring the logs for the new barn and outbuildings. The work was hot but progress was being made

Florence did the usual canning of berries and vegetables from the garden. The girls were a good help but Ken was a pain in the butt as he was into everything. One of the girls had to keep an eye on him all the time.

Before harvest time the first floor walls were taking shape on the house. The logs were ready for the barn and some of the out buildings.

The harvest went well but was not too good of a yield. It was much the same as last year. John and Jack worked with the threshing crews and the weather stayed good for most of the fall.

When it came time for threshing at John's place, the girls stayed home from school to help Florence around the house. They helped take the mid-morning and afternoon snacks to the men. One had to look after Ken all the time. The girls liked this as they thought they were a big help and they were.

The weather stayed dry after the threshing so Jack and Ken kept working on the house while John hauled grain to town and brought in the oat straw to stack by the barn. The wheat straw would be hauled in later as it was needed for bedding in the barn. By mixing the oat straw with the hay, the feed for the stock would go much further. It did not have as much food value but they were not worked that hard in the winter.

Before the snow came, some of the logs were in place for the new barn and the house walls were up for the second floor. They could see no reason why the house and outbuildings could not be finished next year.

Around the first of November, Ken stopped working on the house and said he would be back in the Spring if John needed him. John told him that he was sure that he would be needed and they would be in touch with him.

John and Bart made their trip to the Legion on the eleventh of November. Florence and Dora had a good visit and made plans for Christmas.

By the end of November there was a good amount of snow on the ground. John and Jack were now cutting timber for firewood and lumber. They had a good area cleared where the new farm buildings would be. John even hauled some more pigs to the market.

Around the first of December, John butchered a steer and pig. He also killed a lot of roosters for Florence to can. It was good to have your own meat to go with the vegetables from the garden that had been stored in the root cellar. One could always eat well if they had enough to buy a few things from the store that they could not grow. When you worked all day out in the cold, your appetite was always good.

On the real cold days Jack, worked in the shop making things for the new house. He was now even making cupboards and doors for the closets. He seemed to enjoy trying to make as much as he could ahead of time.

Christmas time was clear and cold but the Mullens and Fords were able to visit over the holiday. Dora was expecting again.

Bart asked John if he had given up on having a bigger family?

John replied with, "I think four is enough to raise now. With the market the way it is sometimes, I think four is too many."

Bart laughed and said, "Yeah, I know, but these things seem to have a way of happening."

Both men laughed at this remark and said no more.

After Christmas, things went as a normal Saskatchewan winter.

There were some real cold days when even the school was closed. But chores still had to be done when you had horses, cows, chickens and pigs.

At the end of February it was a sad time at the Mullen's place. Old Jip, their, dog, had died. He was pretty old but had been a favorite of everyone. He had been the one who had saved Flo when the old sow had attacked her. Everyone had tears in their eyes when John took him away to be buried behind the barn. He had been a good old dog and would be hard to replace.

The Spring wood cutting bee took place as usual. While John was helping at the Campbell farm, Walter said he had heard that John had lost his dog.

John said that he had and would have to get another one sometime.

Walter then said, "My dog just had pups about a month ago. I would give you one if you want. If they are as good as the mother they will make a good farm dog."

John replied, "Yes, Walter, I would take one off your hands. The kids will be really pleased and they still miss old Jip."

When John went home that night and went in the house with a little pup under his arm, the kids went crazy. There was a great argument over what they would call the pup. Everyone had a different name they favoured. It was going to be hard to pick a good one.

Florence finally said, "If there is going to be such a argument over the dog's name, maybe we had better give him back to Walter."

Everything went quiet then Flo said, "It doesn't matter to me what you call the stupid pup. He will never take Jip's place. That dog is the reason I am here. So call him what ever you want to."

Florence raised her eyebrows and said, "That's true Flo, but that does not solve the problem. I think we should call him something that everyone likes."

Just then Ken said, "Nice puppy, black."

Everyone looked at each other and almost said as one, "We will call the pup Blackie."

They all agreed that this was a good name as the pup was as black as coal.

With this major task out of the way, everything was back to normal.

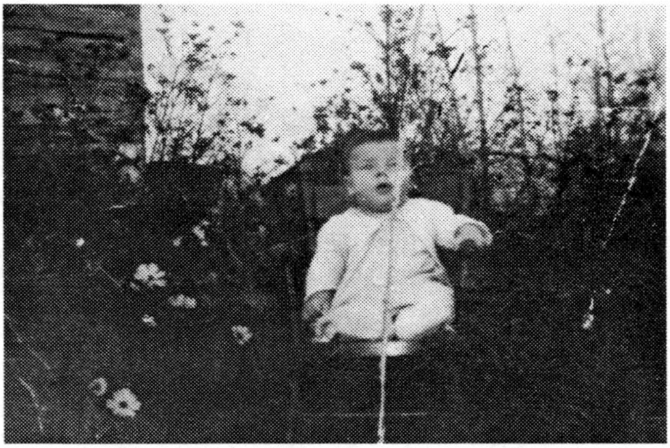

RON FORD 1931

KEN 1932

KEN 1932

JOHN CUTTING ALFALFA

FORD AND MULLEN PICNIC

HARRIEVAL SCHOOL PICNIC

KEN AND HELEN

GOING TO SCHOOL

FLO, AILEEN, HELEN, TEACHER FLORABELLE BENNET AND KEN.

CHAPTER 10

THE NEW HOUSE

In nineteen thirty-five, not many farmers were having land broken. With poor crops and the low price for grain, they were raising more stock and feeding them the grain. John was not going to break any land on his own farm. The last seven acres he broke was not good soil and was full of rocks. Most of the best part of the farm had been broken. What was left was mostly creek beds and rocky soil that was not good for growing grain. It would make good pasture land and still supply the farm with fire wood.

John put in the crop and Jack and Ken worked on the new house. They hoped to have it finished in the Fall. With both of them working it should be all finished.

Florence was trying to train the new pup Blackie to not chase the chickens but to run and bark at any hawks that tried to swoop down and steal the small chicks. She wished that old Jip was still around as he was good at this and would show the pup what to do. It was taking awhile but Blackie was starting to catch on to the idea of chasing the hawks.

John was able to get the hay cut early and twenty acres plowed for summer fallow. After growing grain for three years, it was a good idea to let the soil be black for a year. Sometimes if the Spring was damp, a crop of alfalfa or clover would be planted. When the grass was high enough to mow, a crop of hay would be taken off and the field plowed under. This put nitrogen back into the soil and helped to grow a better crop the next year.

It had been so dry this Spring that it was not worth the chance of trying to grow a crop of hay. John would just spread as much manure as he could on the plowed field.

The kids were getting to be good berry pickers and a good help at weeding the garden. On the hot days Helen and Flo would take tea and sandwiches to Ken and Jack. Sometimes they had to make a trip to the new house and out to the field where John would be working. Some of the places that they had to walk through was just a small roadway with thick trees on both sides. As always, the two sisters had something to fight about. Flo would do the best she could to scare Helen with remarks like, "Did you hear that bear in the bush?" And many other remarks.

Helen would pretend she had not heard what Flo was saying but just the same, she did not feel too safe. When they got back home, Helen would tell Florence what Flo had been doing. Florence could tell that this was bothering Helen.

Florence said in a loud voice so Flo could hear, "I think we will send Flo alone tomorrow if she keeps scaring you, Helen."

Helen replied, "I wasn't scared. I just thought Flo should not do that."

Flo shouted right back, "You were scared, Helen, your eyes were popping right out of Your head."

"Was not," Helen snapped back, nearly in tears. "You couldn't scare anybody."

"Hold it right there," Florence said as she tried to hold back a smile. "Flo, you can be very annoying sometimes and will do anything to get on Helen's nerves. I will tell you what I am going to do. Tomorrow you will go together and if you can't get along, then you will take turns going alone. That way you will not be able to fight and if you are scared, no one will know."

Helen and Flo looked at each other and did not say a word. But you can be sure that there would be no fighting the next day.

That night Florence told John what had happened. John said, "I bet that will keep them quiet for awhile."

They both had a good laugh over this. Even in the tough times there was always a little humour to go around.

On August the eleventh, a Sunday, it was John's birthday. It had been a hot summer so the Fords and Mullens decided to go to Fishing Lake for the day. Jack said he would do the chores and let them have a full day to have some fun for a change.

They got up at four o'clock that morning, loaded the kids and lots of food in the old car and headed off to Ford's farm. Fishing Lake was north-east of Kinistino so they had a fair drive even from the Fords.

It was between six and seven before they got to the lake. They found a spot under the trees and rented a boat. It looked like it was going to be a hot day but what could be better than a good day's fishing and lots of great food in the shade of the trees.?

Bart and John were out on the lake as quick as they could be. The person who ran the little park and rented the boats had told them that over in the south-west corner of the lake was the best fishing. They worked their way up the side of the lake to this spot. They had not been there too long when John caught a pickerel and Bart caught a jack fish.

By noon they had five nice fish in the boat. They went back to the picnic site and as Bart had brought the last of his ice from home, they cleaned the fish and put them on the ice covered with a lot of newspapers in a box.

They then had a big dinner of cold chicken and potato salad. There were a lot of good sweets to go around, also.

After lunch, all the kids had to have a boat ride. After this was done, John and Bart went back fishing. They did very well in the afternoon and were very pleased with their catch. Both of them loved fish so were happy to have done so well.

When they came in for supper they went up to the house to pay for the rent of the boat. They told the man that they were pleased with his advice about where to go on the lake.

The man grinned and said, "Someone told me that a horse had gone through the ice there last winter, so I thought that there would be lots of feed in that area."

They thanked the man and started back to the picnic site.

Bart was the first to speak up. "You know John, I am not too fussy about eating those fish if they have been feeding on a dead horse."

"Oh hell, Bart," John replied. "He just probably told us that so we would give him the fish. Anyway, we aren't going to eat the guts, so what's the difference?"

"Well, I guess you're right", Bart said, "But we bloody well won't tell the women or we won't even get the fish home."

Both men laughed at this and went back to have supper.

The kids had a good swim that afternoon so were tired and ready to go home. Shirley, Dora's latest, was only three months old and was starting to get fussy. Everyone had been up early and were ready to head home.

It was late when the Mullens got home and after everything was put away, everyone was ready for bed. It had been a good day and a nice break away from the farm.

The crops were ready early this year as it had been so dry. They were not good crops again. The dry weather had kept the yield down. Jack did not go to work with the threshing crews. He stayed working on the house. The house was all closed in now and ready for the doors and windows. It was hoped that the Mullens could move in before Christmas. John had got most of the barn finished. The walls were up and the roof covered with poles. He would just put straw on the poles for this winter and put the roof on next year. With the cold dry winters, the barn would be warm and dry.

The chickens and hogs would be left over at the old place. Jack would be staying in the bunkhouse and it would not be too hard to look after them. The stock would still have to be watered at the well by the old place as a new one had not been dug yet. Only the horses being used and the milk cows would be kept over at the new place this winter.

Around the middle of November, Ken was let go but not before Florence had invited him and his family for dinner the next Sunday. Florence told him that he had been a very good worker and that they would never been able to finish the house without him.

Ken grinned and said, "Florence, we will sure be here next Sunday. I have eaten your cooking and I am sure that the family will enjoy it, also. By the way thanks for the compliment. It has been good working with John and Jack."

The next Sunday they had a nice day with Ken's family and it was sort of sad to not have Ken working around the place anymore.

With a lot of hard work and letting some of the other work go, the house was ready to move into on the first of December. This was a big day for the Mullens. Everyone had a job to do. The kids were busy packing up their few belongings into small boxes. When they were ready, they all headed out for the new house. The men were busy moving furniture over so the kids had to walk. They did not mind, but Ken kept dragging his box in the snow. The girls helped as much as they could and they were soon in the house and in a very happy mood.

The furnace downstairs was going and the double drum heater was going in the front room. The kitchen stove was set up and the house was nice and warm.

To keep the upstairs bedrooms warm, a hole was in the ceiling above the big double drum heater. This hole was covered with a grating. Ken had a good time spitting down on the heater below. This didn't last too long after Florence found out what was going on.

Florence looked out the window at the road and saw a large board hanging above the gate. She turned to Jack and said, "What is that out there above the gate?"

Jack grinned and said, "You wanted to call the place "THE HILLCREST FARM" so that is what the sign reads. I hope you like it?"

Florence looked at Jack with tears in her eyes and said in a husky voice, "How can I ever thank you, Jack? You have been so thoughtful. When we get set up here, I will make you an apple pie and we will get some cheese from town as I know that is your favorite."

Jack replied, "Florence, that is payment enough. I will look forward to that day."

The Mullens got settled into the new house and were so pleased with all the room. The view from the top floor windows was really nice. One could see most of the farms for miles. In the morning you could see the smoke coming from the farm houses. Some days you had to scrape the frost from inside the windows to see out. I guess that they would have to check each day to see if their neighbours were up and around.

It was a good move and everyone was happy in the new house.

CHAPTER 11

FIRST WINTER, NEW HOUSE

After the first few days, the excitement of the new house started to wear off. This house was much bigger and in the cold weather it would cool down much faster than the log house.

The fire would be out in the morning and the house was real cold. John said he would have to get some coal for the downstairs furnace so it would last all night. It was a small furnace but would help keep the chill off overnight. The big double forty-five gallon drums would sure throw the heat but would not last the night. Sometimes John would get up in the night and fill the stove again. Many nights it was so nice in bed that the stove was forgotten. Then it would be hustling around in the morning to light the fires in the kitchen stove, the big drum stove and the furnace in the basement. No one else seemed to move until the house was warm.

The full basement had a big sand box in one corner. The vegetables were buried in the sand to keep them from freezing. The furnace was in the centre of the floor. The cream separator was over in the corner with a bench to keep all the containers. Most of the other side of the basement was full of wood for all the stoves. The kitchen stove and furnace took short pieces while the drum stove took wood up to three feet long.

Florence liked the new house. She had a big kitchen and a dining room with a big table. She would have to get a good set of furniture some day. Jack had built a nice sized table that would have to do for a while.

The kids had a little farther to go to school but they could cut through past the old house so it wasn't much difference. There was still stock at the old place so it didn't seem too lonely. Jack was still living in the bunkhouse but the house looked empty and sad.

Jack and John were kept busy with the stock and trying to cut wood for next year. They also would put skids under some of the buildings at the old place and haul them over to the new place before the snow went. There would not be many saw logs cut as there was still lumber left over. Wood cutting, ice cutting and moving the buildings over would come first.

The Mullens and Fords had a good Christmas and New Years get together. Florence was real pleased to show off the new house and have lots of room for everyone. The kids could be in the large living room and not be under foot in the kitchen.

Dora said to Florence, "You know, Florence, if we ever have to give up our farm, we will come and live with you. You sure have lots of room here!"

Florence grinned and replied, "Yes, it sure is nice having all this room but it sure gets cool fast when the heat is off."

Dora nodded and said, "I think I could stand that. Your view of the valley is so nice. I can sure see why you built up here. You can even see the trains at Ethelton and Pathlow when they go through.

"Yes," Florence answered. "The trains look like snakes going along the tracks blowing up steam from their heads. It is hard to believe it is five and six miles away. On a clear frosty night the lights in Melfort show up like a mirage and that is twenty-five miles by road."

"I bet the northern lights are pretty at night?" Dora said. "You should be able to see them for miles."

"Oh, they are beautiful." Florence replied. "The whole horizon is lit up sometimes. Too bad it is so cold or one could stand outside and watch them."

"Speaking of watching," Dora questioned. "Where did the men go?"

"Oh, down to the barn, I guess." Florence answered, "You know they say they are looking at the stock. But we both know it's the bottle hidden there that they go to see. They should know every hair on the stock by now."

Both women had a good laugh at this, then Dora said, "Why don't they just keep it in the basement and then they would not have as far to go each time?"

"Gosh, Dora don't, suggest that!." Florence retorted, "It would be too close then and they might never make it up the stairs for supper. The barn is further away at this place and it gives them some exercise."

Again they had a good laugh.

After the holidays were over it was back to the work of running a farm in the winter.

Most of the smaller buildings were moved over to the new place. The meat house, shop and a small feed shed had been moved. The Most of the stock were still at the old place as that was where the well was. When John went over in the morning to water the team that he kept at the new place, he would bring back a barrel or so of water for the milk cows. In the Spring they would have to dig a well by the new place. They had been so busy getting ready to move in that they had not thought about the need for a well.

A new pig pen were being built and chicken houses. These were made of squared logs and lumber roofs. Lots of days it was too cold to work on these buildings, which didn't matter as they would not be used until spring when the well would be dug after the ground was not frozen.

Things went fine, when in March, John said to Jack, "I'm tired of going over to the old place twice a day and bringing water back for the milk cows. What do you say we build a big fire down next to the creek above the barn? We can use all the brush and limbs we have here. That should melt the ground and we can start digging now."

Jack replied, "It would be worth a try and as soon as we get though the frost, it would be easy digging."

Jack and John hauled all the wood to be burnt and piled it down by the creek. This creek only ran a bit in the Spring when the snow melted. The well would be back a ways-just above the creek bed.

When the men had piled all the wood to be burned, they set it on fire. They hauled more over as they wanted the fire to burn all night. While the fire was burning, they made up a frame with a pulley at the top. They would mount this over where the well was going to be, and with a rope through the pulley and a bucket at the end, one man would be up top and be able to pull the dirt up.

The fire was kept going all night and in the morning the men were ready to start work digging the well. It would be four feet square so they would have room to dig when it got deeper.

The men started digging as soon as they could. They made good time the first few feet as the frost was out of the soil and the dirt was sandy. When they stopped in the afternoon, they were deep enough to start using the bucket and pulley system the next day.

Jack said to John, "You know that ground will freeze again over night if we don't do something. I think if we put a few boards over the top and some straw, over them it will stop it from freezing.

John replied, "Hell of an idea, Jack. That will save us time in the morning. Let's do it right now."

The men covered the well then went to do the night chores.

The next few days the men continued to dig the well. It was slow work but they spent as much time at it as they could.

When they got down to twelve feet, they built a square crib out of boards and lowered it down the well. This kept the dirt from falling in and made it a lot safer. They did this again every five feet. The well was down now just over twenty feet deep. The men were starting to think that soon they might hit some water coming in from the sides.

One morning when Jack went down for his turn to dig below he yelled up to John.

"Hey, John, there is water coming in around the side. Not much, but it is collecting at the bottom."

John yelled back, "God, it is about time! Let's keep going for another five feet or so."

They kept digging until the water was coming in faster than they could keep it dry. They were about five feet below where it had started coming in, so they quit and put the cover over the well.

The next morning when they checked, there was a good five or six feet of water in the well. They lowered the bucket down and pulled out a lot of water and dumped it out. They could not seem to haul it fast enough to make the well go dry.

John and Jack were elated that the well seemed to be giving a good supply of water. The water smelled good and was quite clear. They would draw some more water in the afternoon and see how they made out.

Jack made a cover for the well with a small trap door for the bucket to go down. This also made the well safe so the kids would not fall in.

If the well worked out, they would move the pump over from the other place and then the stock could be moved over. That would make for easier times when doing the chores.

The new well worked out fine and the stock was moved over to the new place. The pump and watering trough was moved over and the stock was now all at the new place. Jack stayed over in the bunkhouse for he liked having his own place alone.

Things had gone well this first winter in the new house. Everyone was happy. If only the price of grain and other farm products would go up, then it would be a lot better.

John and Florence could only hope this would happen soon.

CHAPTER 12

SPRING 1936

April in 1936 came in mild. The snow started to go and the runoff filled the new well to the top. What logs that had been cut had been hauled to be cut into lumber. The rest had been cut up into firewood. The ice house was full and covered with sawdust. It looked like the next thing to do was get the machines ready for Spring planting. Jack and John worked on this in the shop and had everything ready when the soil was ready to work.

The garden was plowed first and planted. The fields were done next. With the early thaw it looked like another dry summer.

When the crop was all planted, the weather was still dry. John had got some paint and was ready to do the house. With Jack's help, it would not take too long to do this job.

One day when they were painting the house, a car came into the driveway and stopped at the house. A man got out that John knew was the station agent at Melfort. He came over to where John and Jack were working and said, "Good day."

John got down from the ladder he was working on and went over and said, "Good day, Mr. Parnell. What can we do for you?"

"Hello, John," Mr. Parnell said. "Please call me Dave. I have come to see you about your hired hand Jack. I have heard that he is a real good carpenter and would like to know if I could talk you into letting him come work for me?"

"Well," John said, "I guess we will have to talk about this."

Dave nodded his head and said, “I would like that very much.”

John replied, “Well, if it involves Jack, he had better be with us.”

Dave agreed and John called Jack to join them in the house for a cup of coffee. There was always hot water and time for a cup of coffee or tea.

John took the men into the house and told Florence what was going on. She put the coffee pot on the stove and the men sat around the dining room table.

Dave was the first to speak. “John, you have a real nice house here. With the paint job, it will be something you should be proud of. I would like a house built for me and that is why I have come to see you.”

John nodded and said, “Yes we are proud of our house but with times the way they are, it gets harder to get ends to meet.”

Dave nodded his head in agreement and said, “I agree and my reason for being here is to see if Jack could come work for me and build a house. I know he did everything but make the glass, so it would be to my advantage to have him build my house.”

John waited a minute then said, “Jack is a real good worker and his workmanship is good. I would hate to lose him but I can not keep him on much longer. The money is so tight right now and the price of our products so low. It is up to Jack, but I would like to keep him until after the hay is in.”

Jack spoke up at this time and said, “John, I have liked working with you and I know you are hurting. You gave me a job when I was down and out. You should be able to handle things after the hay is in. I will stay until the house is painted and the hay in, then go work for Dave here. I don’t want to leave but I understand what the times have dictated. I will miss the kids, you and your wife. You have treated me like one of the family and I will never forget that. What do you say to that, Dave?”

Dave said, "If that is O.K. with you and John that is fine with me. Also, if you are stuck and need a hand for a while, just come and get Jack to help you when needed."

The men finished their coffee and agreed that Jack would go to Melfort and build Dave's house after the house was painted and the hay was in.

The men went outside, shook hands and the deal was sealed.

Florence sat in the house with her cup of coffee and wondered what the kids would feel like with Jack leaving. He was the last of the men to go and had been so good with the kids. She would have to break it to them gently as they thought a lot of Jack.

The painting went well and the hay was mowed and stacked behind the barn ready for winter feed.

The night before Jack left, there was a big dinner made. Florence roasted a couple of chickens and baked an apple pie with cheese. This was Jack's favorite. He had two pieces and this made Florence happy.

Flo spoke up and said, "I guess you will come back and see us, Jack, if Mom will bake you an apple pie with cheese?"

Jack cleared his throat and replied, "Flo, I would come back and see you any day without the apple pie. But if it was here, I sure would not turn it down. I promise you I will be back to see you. Maybe I will come out on Thanksgiving and see you all. I think that would be fitting for what you have done for me."

Florence then spoke up and said, "I think I can say for both John and I that you have more than done your share and you are welcome at our house any time."

It was John's turn to speak. "Hey, before we all start crying in our tea, let's wish Jack the best at his new job. I will drive him to the five o'clock train tomorrow night. If the kids want to come along after school, then they better hurry home."

The kids all spoke at once and said they would be home right after school so they could see Jack away on the train. It would be a sad day but would all work out in the long run.

The next day Jack was taken to the train and all the kids said good-bye to him. They would miss him but were glad that he had a job to go to.

The berry picking this year was not too good. The summer was dry again and the only thing that kept the garden going was that John hauled water from the new well and kept the vegetables in a good supply of water. The grain crop was looking poor again and the only hope was that the price of pork would stay up as they had a good bunch of pigs that they could sell in the Fall.

This year John had planted about two acres of turnips. They would be mixed with the grain and fed to the pigs. They had to be cut up but made the feed go farther. Some would be stored in the basement but most of them would be kept in a spare stall at the back of the barn to keep them from freezing. Some would be kept outside until the cold weather came. They had to be watered as the weather was so dry. This meant hauling water in barrels at least once a week, but they were growing good.

With Jack gone, the days were busy and soon Fall was coming and harvest time.

Helen would be going into grade nine and plans had been made for her to board at the Stevenson place close to the high school in Ethelton. This was the closest high school and six miles each way was too far to travel, especially in the winter time. This would add extra costs, but something would be worked out. Helen was so good with books, she just had to continue her schooling.

The harvest was early again as the summer had been hot and dry. The yield was poor so as before, John sold the good grain and bought cheaper grades to feed the stock. A few dollars were made this way, but not a lot.

All the garden had been brought in for storage and canning. The turnips had been the biggest job. They used the wagon with the box on and drove it down the rows and threw the turnips into the box. John and Florence would walk along beside the wagon and Ken, five now, would ride up on the seat and hold the reins of the two horses. They did not have to be steered, but he felt real important as he was helping with the harvest. John would go to the front of the team at the end of the rows and turn them around to start another trip down the rows. The horses started and stopped on command from John. The only reason Ken was on the wagon was to keep him from running around and getting in the way. He did not know this and was real happy with his job.

Helen had settled in at her boarding place and liked it fine. The harvest was completed and now things were being done to get ready for another winter.

John and Florence were pleased with what they had done so far this year. The house looked nice and the harvest was in. Now the long winter was ahead and they hoped they would do as well.

CHAPTER 13

WINTER 1936-37

In September, the Mullens got a letter from Jack saying he would like to spend Thanksgiving with them. They were pleased to hear this and the kids were overjoyed.

When John went to Ethelton on his next trip, he phoned Dave Parnell in Melfort and said he could pick Jack up in Ethelton at the eight o'clock train on Saturday, October the 10th. He would take him to the five o'clock train on Tuesday the thirteenth. He had to pick up Helen and return her for school, so that would work out fine for him.

Dave said that would be good. Jack had been working real hard and could stand a day or two off to get away to a different place.

Both were happy with the arrangement that had been set up.

When John went to the store to get his supplies, he picked up a box of apples and a big slab of cheese. He knew Florence would be cooking up a lot of apple pies because they were Jack's favorite. Being from Nova Scotia, John liked apples of any kind.

On the Saturday before Thanksgiving, John picked up Jack at the train and Helen from the Stevensons. They had a good trip home as the weather was nice. They did a lot of talking and the trip went by real fast.

When they got home, supper was a little late but no one cared as they were enjoying each other's company. The kids had to be held back as they were asking Jack questions all at the same time. They were told they would all get a chance after supper. With this, they left Jack alone for the rest of the meal.

After John had done the chores, they all sat down to enjoy some time with Jack. He told them that the house he was building was going well. The walls were up and the roof was on. As soon as the chimney was finished, he would board up all the windows and all but one door. They would put in a double drum heater and he would use the house as a shop for the winter. He could make up all the window and door frames and be warm at the same time.

Everyone thought this made good sense as then he could work all winter in comfort.

They talked late into the night, even after the kids had gone to bed. They had so much to tell each other. It was nice to see Jack again.

Jack told them that he had seen and heard from some of the men in Flin Flon. They were all still working in the mine. They had told him to say hello to the Mullens. They didn't mind the work but missed Florence's home cooking. This made Florence smile, for she had also missed the working crew.

Not much work was done around the farm that weekend just the chores that had to be done each day. Jack and John had many good games of crib and ate many great meals.

The big turkey dinner was held on Monday as Tuesday,,Jack had to catch the five o'clock train back to Melfort.

John had traded some chickens for three turkeys, so they still had two left for Christmas. Maybe they would have one on November the eleventh if things went right and the Fords could come over.

On Tuesday, John was getting the team ready to drive Helen to her boarding place and Jack to the train. Everyone was saying their goodbyes to Jack. When the kids were finished saying goodbye to Jack, he went over to Florence and put his arms around her and gave her a big hug. Then he said, "Florence, you have been the mother that I never had. You have been so good to me and your apple pie is the best in the world."

Florence looked at Jack and replied in a husky voice, "Jack, you are welcome at our house any time. Make sure you come back whenever you can."

Just then Ken said, "Mom must have something in her eyes as they have tears in them."

This broke the tension and everyone had a good laugh.

John came along with the team and soon they were on their way. It had been a great weekend that they would all remember for a long time.

Now it was time to get back to running the farm. A lot of work still had to be done. John and Florence would be busy for the next while.

The next thing John was going to do was get the old bunk house ready to move over to the new place. He would bring it over in two halves. The shop part he would leave as is. The other part he would use as a grain storage for the pigs and chickens. He would put the stove into the shop so he could repair harness and anything else that could be done inside where it would be warm.

November the eleventh was on a Wednesday that year, so the Fords came to the Mullens for a turkey dinner. They picked Helen up and brought her home as their farm was only a quarter of a mile from the Stevenson's farm. John and Bart didn't go to Pathlow this year. They decided to stay at home and do a little celebrating there. That would mean many trips to the barn. They beat this by having a fire in the shop stove and spending time there. John had moved the shop over and now only had the bunk house left to move.

Bart offered to help John move the bunk house but John told him that it was already up on skids and with the snow on the ground and with four horses, it would come over easy. He was going to move it between the pig pen and the chicken coop. This way he would not have to pack the feed as far as now. It was big enough to hold grain and some turnips.

Bart liked John's workshop. It had a stove, work bench and shelves for storing equipment and tools. He had put it in a rock base to mount the small forge. The foot pedal driven grindstone was mounted in one corner.

John and Bart spent most of the afternoon in the shop until Ken and Ron came down and told them it was supper time. The women had a good visit and the young people were having a good time playing games and talking about old times.

After supper, the Fords left and told the Mullens that they would see them for Christmas at their house. They would take Helen there on Christmas Eve and that would save them a trip to pick her up. Helen did not want to miss Christmas Eve at home, but it seemed the best thing to do at that time of year.

The rest of November was cold and there was a lot of snow. Florence was kept busy with the housework and helping the two girls with theirhome work at night. John kept busy moving the bunk house and getting it ready for a grain shed. The water trough had to be chopped out twice a day to water the stock. It was a good job the well was close to the stock.

The Mullens spent Christmas with the Fords and brought Helen home with them. The weather turned real cold just before New Year's . The Fords made it over for New Year's Day but took Helen back with them to save John the trip in the cold weather.

Helen had got her first report from school and was at the top of her class. All John said was,. "You will make a hell of a school marm one of these days."

Florence had a little nicer praise and knew they were doing the right thing sending her to high school. It was worth the extra cost.

The weather stayed cold so John and Bart cut ice and hauled it to their ice sheds. It seemed silly to cut and haul ice at this time of the year, but it sure was nice in early summer to be able to make your own ice cream and many other things that required ice.

John cut some smaller trees for wood and piled it in the yard not far from the house. This made it easy to throw into the basement window. This was Ken's job. He had to pile it up after it had been thrown in. He also had to collect the eggs each day-a job that he hated. Florence explained to him that everyone had to do their part on a farm. Ken said that he didn't mind doing his part but why did it have to be with the chickens?

Florence asked, "Why do you hate chickens so much?"

Ken replied with, "They stink and when I try to get the eggs from underneath them, they peck my hand with their beaks."

Florence held back a laugh and said, "I will make you a small size of gloves from some of Dad's old ones. They are made of leather and the beaks won't hurt you. What do you think of that?"

Ken answered, "That might be O.K. Now I won't have to rap them on the side of the head when they peck me."

Florence did laugh this time and said, "No wonder they peck you. I am glad now to make the gloves. Maybe the chickens won't get brain damage from your rapping them on the side of the head."

Most everything went well for the rest of the winter. Spring was starting to come and some of the trees were in bud. The ground was showing up where the snow had melted.

One night Florence and John were having a late night cup of cocoa after the children had gone to bed.

Florence looked at John and said, "Do you think we can stand another dry summer like we have been getting in the past?"

John shook his head and replied, "I don't think so. The snow leaves early and we don't get any rain during the summer. Do you know some of the farms in the south have lost all their top soil to the wind? I have never seen it so dry and windy since we moved here. We are lucky as our fields are protected from most of the wind by trees. But even some of the farmers by Ethelton have lost top soil because they cut down all their trees."

They both agreed that they were lucky to still have their farm as a lot of people had lost theirs with the depression and all. John said he was lucky to be getting the pension from the war even, if it had cost him one lung.

With this Florence and John went to bed, thankful that they had a good house, a farm to keep them in food and a great family. It was hard work, but some day it might just pay off.

CHAPTER 14

ANOTHER DRY SUMMER

The snow went very fast in the spring of 1937. Even now, the soil had big cracks in it where the dirt had dried up fast. When planting the crop, the air was full of dust and the temperature was high for this time of the year. Things were not starting out too good.

The farmers were hoping on hope that there would be some rain, but it never came. The crop was slow coming up and was way behind time in growing. The weather was very hot and the wind seemed to blow all the time.

John did not plant any alfalfa or clover this year as it would never grow to anything in this dry soil. The creek dried up in June over in the pasture and the stock had to come to the well for water. This was putting a strain on the well and it soon might just run out of water. He may have to haul water from the old well over at the first house.

Most of the wild berries dried up before they got to any size. It was going to be a bad year for canning. It was a good thing that Florence still had some canned fruit from the year before.

The well dried up before the end of June. The second well over at the old house dried up in the middle of July. The garden was kept watered, but John had to haul water from the creek that ran behind the school. A lot of the farmers were hauling water from this creek. They were lucky that this water supply had not dried up. John had put four forty-five gallon drums in the wagon box and hauled his water that way. Even with a canvas cover over the top, the steel wheels were so rough that a lot of the water was spilled before he got back to the farm.

One night when he and Florence were talking about the lack of water,he said to her, "You know, Florence, I think I am going to drive the old car to Mike's and have him make me up a Bennett buggy. That way I won't spill as much water as it will have rubber tires to run on."

These wagons were called that because R. B. Bennett was the Prime Minister of Canada from 1930 to 1935. A lot of the farmers had converted their cars over to rubber-tired wagons. They could not afford to run their cars, so did the next best thing. The Prime Minister must be the reason why they were in a Depression, so they called the wagon after him.

Florence thought for a minute then said, "You have not got a licence for the car, so how are you going to get it to Mike's?"

John just grinned and said, "Who the hell is going to stop a poor old farmer that is getting his car made into a Bennett buggy? Anyway, the nearest police station is twenty-five miles away. They probably don't have enough money to patrol all the little farm roads."

Florence just shook her head and said, "I didn't hear a word you said."

The next day he tried to start the old car. It took him two days to get it going.

The next day, he tied a horse behind the car and set off to Mike's place. He did not see a soul and got there with no problems.

Mike came out to see John and said, "How can you afford to run a car? Did you find gold on your place?"

John laughed and replied, "No Mike, I just drove it down here to see if you would make me up a Bennett buggy. If you take the engine and transmission and anything else not needed to convert this thing,

I think we could make an even trade.

Mike shook his head and said, "John, I have to show some kind of a profit so you will have to give me something to boot."

John just shook his head and replied, "Mike, I don't have much to offer. Times are not what they used to be."

Mike grinned and said, "John, I hear there are some new apples in from B.C. and your wife makes real good apple pies. You bring me a couple of pies and a couple of chickens cleaned and ready to cook and we have a deal."

John looked at Mike and said, "You drive a hard bargain but I think that we can live with that. You know you had me scared for awhile. But that is not too much to ask."

Both men shook hands and the bargain was sealed.

John went home happy as now he would have a wagon that would ride smooth. It would ride better and when he had to deliver eggs to the train on frozen ground, there would be less chance of breakage.

When John got home, he told Florence what he had done. She replied with, "So you left me with all the work to be done. I'll bet you want me to kill and clean the chickens also?"

"No," John said. "I will look after the chickens. That's what you get for being such a good apple pie maker."

Florence just grinned and said, "Flattery will do the trick every time."

They both laughed at this as there wasn't much to laugh at anymore.

A few days later John took a team down to Mike's place. He rode one horse and led the other behind. He had two apple pies in a box and two chickens he had killed and cleaned that morning. It was difficult carrying the pies on horseback but he got there with them in good shape.

Mike came out to meet John and said, "I hope those pies are in good shape. I wouldn't want them all broken up."

John looked at Mike and replied, "You know I would not deliver you anything that was not in good shape. I hope my Bennett buggy is in as good as shape as the pies are."

Mike laughed and said, "I guess that is a saw-off. I think we both will be happy with what we get."

Both men had a chuckle over this and then got down to what they had to do.

John hooked the team up to the Bennett buggy and everything looked fine. Mike took the chickens and pies into the house and came back out.

The men seemed happy with what they had got and talked for a while.

Then Mike said, "John, I can't stand here shooting the bull. I have to get over to the store and buy some cheese to go with the apple pies. My wife is cooking up the chicken and I can hardly wait for supper. It is a good thing that we can trade with each other. I have not cut a lot of lumber for awhile and I only have a small garden. You farmers help keep me in food for the work that I do. If we can keep this up maybe we will beat this Depression."

John nodded his head and replied, "Mike, we have got to stick together to beat this thing. If we do not lose our sense of humour, then all will not be lost."

Mike came right back with, "John, we have had a lot of good deals in the past that were good for both of us. Let's keep it that way and we will fight our way through this damn Depression."

Both men agreed and shook hands.

John went home with his Bennett buggy and was real proud when he showed it to Florence and the kids. They all thought it would be a asset to the farm and were happy.

The hauling of the water was much easier now. There was less spillage and more water got to where it should.

The hay crop had been poor and John would have to use a lot

of straw this winter. The stock would suffer but what else could a person do?

The harvest was early and not very good. John used the Bennett buggy to haul his grain to town. Mike had made a good job as the wagon box fit on perfect. He had even mounted the spare tire underneath on the bar between the back and front wheels. Behind the draw bar in the front of the wagon was a steel box with the hand air pump, tools and a patching kit. Yes, Mike had done a real good job.

Ken started school this Fall. He made a real good impression the first day. He was sitting in the first row, the second from the front. The boy in front of him had waited until the teacher had turned her back and then had turned around and stabbed Ken in the hand with his pencil. After Ken got over the shock of what had happened, he reached ahead and gave the boy's ear a real good yank. Just then, the teacher turned around and the boy screamed.

The teacher came over and pulled Ken out of the seat and said, "We will not have any of this kind of thing going on in my classroom. And just to show you all that I mean what I say, Ken is going to get the strap for pulling Jim's ear. So Ken, you go into the cloakroom and wait for me."

It seemed like an hour before the teacher came in and Ken was getting real scared. When she came in, she made Ken put both hands out in front of him. The teacher then gave him two whacks with the strap on both hands. Then she said, "Maybe that will make you think before you do something that stupid again."

Ken went back to his desk but refused to cry. His hands stung like heck but he just bit his lip and thought about how he could pay Jim Woods back for what he had done.

Flo and Aileen could not wait to get home and tell their mother what had happened. Ken dragged behind all the way home.

When the girls had finished telling Florence, they both asked

"What are you going to do about it, Mom?"

Florence just told them to go outside and send Ken in to see her.

When Ken came in the house, Florence said to him, "I hear you were bad in school today. What have you got to say for yourself?"

Ken looked at her and said, "Well, Jim Woods stabbed me in the hand with his pencil and I just wanted to let him know he couldn't get away with that. I got caught and he didn't."

Florence shook her head and replied, "Well, maybe you have learned your lesson, so I won't punish you anymore."

Ken looked at her with big eyes and said, "Do I have to go back to school tomorrow or can I stay home now?"

Florence had to grin and say, "Yes, you have to go back to school tomorrow and for a long time to come. Now go out and do your chores before supper."

That night when John and Florence were alone, she told him the story about Ken's first day in school. She had told the girls not to tell their Dad as he just might give Ken a licking, also. When she had finished the story, she waited to see what John would say.

John just shook his head and said, "He sure is a stubborn little bugger with a mind of his own. He must have got that from the Sabine side of the family."

Florence looked at John and said, "Yes, and if you keep that up, you will find out just how stubborn we can be."

They looked at each other, laughed, and went to bed.

CHAPTER 15

MORE OF THE SAME

The Fall work in 1937 was about the same as any other year. Helen had gone back to school and now all the kids were in school. It was so quiet around the big house that Florence would sing a lot just to keep herself company.

On one of his trips to town, John found enough money to buy new batteries for the radio. It would give Florence company and also they could listen to the hockey games on Saturday night. There were some good programs that came on at night and the range that could be picked up was great. What better way to spend the long dark winter nights?

It rained hard for a few days at the end of September, but it was only about three months too late. One good thing, the well filled with water again and this cut down a lot of work of hauling water. There was an early snowfall in October and then a mild spell that melted all the snow. This also helped to put more water in the soil and wells.

On Sunday, October the eleventh, the day before Thanksgiving, Jack showed up at the farm with Dave Parnell's car. He said he had just dropped in to say hello and tell them that he had finished the house and was going back home to Ontario to live.

Florence said, " No way is he going to get off that easy. You just drive into town and phone Dave and tell him you have been asked to stay over to have dinner with us tomorrow. And while you are in town, you can pick up some cheese and apples. I will give you the money and Mrs. Boyd will open up for you. She would never turn down a chance to make a few cents."

Jack thought for a minute then replied, "I will do that, Florence. I don't think Dave will mind as they had not planned to go anywhere. As for the money, I will get the stuff and you can make the pies and that will be fair enough."

The roads had dried out after the rain and snow so Jack was no time before he got back with the apples and cheese. And Dave had said it was O.K. for him to stay overnight and come back the next day.

Jack also added with a smile, "You were right, Florence, Mrs. Boyd was glad to make a few cents."

They both laughed at this and began making plans for the next day. Helen had come home and brought a friend with her. There would be eight for dinner so they had better have a big pork roast and at least a couple of chickens for supper. John could kill the chickens and clean them in the morning while she cooked the roast from the pig they had butchered last week.

The next morning, Florence was up early to prepare everything for the two meals. She would bake the pies first and put them out in the cooler, then cook the roast for dinner. After dinner, she would cook the chickens for supper. It was a lot of work, but it was nice to have all the family around, and Jack, with Helen's friend, would add to the making of a good day.

Helen's friend Betty was the daughter of Mrs. Boyd that ran one of the stores in Ethelton. She and Helen had been close since they started high school the year before. They were only about a quarter of a mile from each other, so spent a lot of time together. She was also a good help around the house and was helping Florence today.

The Thanksgiving meals went well and everyone had a good visit. After supper, Jack drove Helen and Betty back to Ethelton as it was on his way to Melfort. This would save John making the trip early the next morning.

Later that night, John and Florence were talking over the weekend. They both agreed that it was nice to have the family together and with Jack there, it made for a good time. They would miss Jack but hoped that he would do well back east. It didn't matter where you went now jobs, were just about impossible to find. The Depression was hard on everyone. It seemed that every time John went to town, he heard of someone else that had given up their farm and moved on. He and Florence wondered if they could make ends meet much longer. Thank God for the small pension, for without that, they would have gone under a long time ago.

For the next while, the weather switched between rain and snow. It never got real cold, but it would come soon.

Florence was canning up chickens and some of the pork. John had held off butchering a steer as the weather was not too cold and he wanted to wait until it was cold enough to freeze the meat in the shed. It was cold enough at night to keep the pork, but he did not want to take a chance of losing the beef.

By the first week in November, it turned cold and Bart and John did not go to the Legion on the eleventh. They decided to wait until Christmas and New Year's and see if the weather was better.

John had made repairs to the roof of his barn. Some of the poles had rotted and he replaced them and put more straw on the roof. He had never had time to build the new barn and was making the old one do for now. He butchered a steer and hung it in the shed. He also hauled about forty pigs to market. The price was not high but would help out. The feed for the hogs was not much, it was just the work involved, but that did not cost anything.

Ken had seemed to settle into school for now. From what Flo and Aileen had said, he and Jim Woods had been in a good fight after school one day. Jim ended up with a bloody nose and ran home crying. Now they seemed to be the best of friends. This was all for the better as they had to go to school together for the next few years.

The weather stayed very cold until just before Christmas. The Fords and Mullens went back and forth for the holidays and had the usual good time. They looked forward to this time together so much, it would have been sad if the weather had prevented their time together.

John and Bart made plans for the ice cutting and also Bart was short of trees on his quarter section. He was going to come up to John's and they would cut wood together. Harvey, Bart's oldest son, could look after the place and Bart would just stay and cut wood all week. This would work out well as it was nice to have two people when working in the bush as you never knew when something could happen and you would be all by yourself.

Most everything went well for the rest of the winter and everyone was looking forward to Spring. It would be nice to see green grass again after a long cold winter.

CHAPTER 16

BAD SUMMER 1938

When the spring break-up came in 1938, it warmed up very fast. There had been a good deal of snow and the fields got a good soaking when it melted.

The crops were put in a little earlier this year and came up fast. Around the first week of June, it rained for a few days. It looked like there would be a good harvest this year.

The garden was coming well and the wild berries had a good yield. Florence and the girls did well picking and canning. With the girls out of school, they were a good help. Ken hung around his Dad most of the time. He could be of some help when John needed something in the field from the shop. Sometimes it might just be a wrench or something to repair a broken piece of harness on the horses.

By the middle of July, the weather was very hot. It did not even cool down at night. There would be a few clouds come up every once in awhile but no rain ever fell. It was so hot working in the fields doing summer fallow that John and Ken would get some turnip leaves and pour water over them and put them under their straw hats. This helped keep a person a little cooler.

The hay crop was fair and there would be enough to put them through the winter. John did not keep any more stock than he needed. He would sell off or trade any he could.

One afternoon, John was harrowing the summer fallow when he

looked up and saw a huge black cloud coming toward them from the north-west. Just then, the wind started to pick up real strong.

John stopped the four horses and hollered at Ken, "Come help me unhook the horses. We have got to get to the barn as fast as we can. There is a hell of a storm coming!"

They got the horses unhitched and John grabbed Ken and threw him up on one of the outside horses. He yelled at him to hang on and jumped up onto the other outside horse.

They hurried toward the barn as fast as they could. Ken was hanging onto his horse's harness hames to help stay on. He was used to riding horses, but not quite in this fashion.

When they got to the barn, they both jumped off and unhooked the horses from each other. They were starting to get a bit uneasy as the wind was now starting to howl with a good force.

They just put the horses in their stalls and did not even tie them up. They closed the barn door and with John holding Ken's hand, they ran for the house.

When they got inside, John yelled, "Everyone head for the basement."

Florence had already taken the children downstairs and was just coming up to see if John and Ken had made it in from the field. She saw them come in and they all went down into the basement.

It was only about two-thirty in the afternoon but it was almost totally dark. It was going to be a bad storm.

Everyone stood together in the middle of the basement. You could hear the wind blowing outside even though they were ten feet below ground level. The basement windows were small as there was only two feet of wall above the ground.

Next you could hear the soil and junk hitting the windows and sounded like they might break. You could now taste the grit that was coming in any small cracks or openings.

Then the thunder and lightning started. Even with only four small windows,it would light up the whole basement just as bright as day. The thunder was so loud that it was hard on the ears. It must have been real close as even the ground shook beneath their feet. Next, there was a roar that could be heard on the roof two floors above. This lasted for about twenty minutes and then everything went all quiet.

They waited for a few minutes and then John said, "I am going up and take a look and see if it's okay. for everyone to go upstairs."

John went up and soon hollered down that the storm had passed and it was safe to come up. It was light out again and you would never know from inside that there had been a storm. Everything was covered with dust and you could still taste it in your mouth.

John and Florence went outside and could not believe what they saw. A big black cloud was off in the distance and the sun was shining. John looked at Florence and said. "Jesus H. Christ, we have been ruined. Just look at that. "

Florence replied, "For once I agree with you John. Half of our place has been blown away. What the heck are we going to do now?"

The whole family just stood there in awe as they looked over the damage that had been done. There was hail all over the ground so thick you could not see the grass. Some of the hail stones were as big as an apple. They had rolled down the slope of the back yard and piled up against the hedge at the bottom at least a foot or more deep.

As they looked around, they could see that the outhouse was gone. The four chicken coops had no roofs. The chickens had gone into roost when it had got dark and they could see some of them sitting on the poles. The barn maybe had lost some straw from the roof but otherwise looked alright from a distance. The pig pen and other sheds being low and in the trees were still standing.

When one looked from left to right, it seemed like a big mower had come across from corner to corner of the farm. It would take some time to figure out all the damage.

Ken had gone down by the hedge and was making snowballs and throwing them at the girls. There was a lot of screaming and yelling going on.

Florence looked at John and said, "It must be nice to be able to not worry about things like what has just happened. Look at that kid. He can make a game out of anything."

John shook his head and replied, "He won't think it so funny when we have to go hungry this winter after what we have just lost."

Florence nodded her head and added, "That is for sure. I will get the girls started at cleaning up the house. There must be an inch of dust and dirt on everything. Then I will come with you and we will look over the damage more closely."

John walked to the chicken coops to wait for Florence. Ken had followed and was looking into the coops with his dad. They could see a lot of dead chickens on the floor. They must have been hit with big hail stones after the roof had blown off. John looked at Ken and said,

"Well, son, there is your first job. Pick up all the dead chickens and take them down to the manure pile. They will have to be buried, so dig a hole to put them in. Keep track of how many are dead. That should keep you busy for a while."

Ken turned up his nose and said, "If we leave them there, maybe the wild animals will pack them away and I won't have to bury them."

John snapped back, "We are not going to wait for that, so snap to it right now."

Ken went away to the manure pile by the barn to start digging a hole. All of a sudden, farm life didn't seem so good.

Florence came back and told John that the house was in a real mess. Even the beds would have to be stripped and the blankets shook out to get rid of the grit. The girls will be busy for a long time. "By the way, where is Ken?"

John laughed for the first time and told her what he was doing.

Even Florence had to grin as she thought about how happy he would be.

As Florence and John were looking over the rest of the damage, they made plans of what they would do next. They would have to build another outhouse. In the meantime, the women would use the one in the basement that was used in the wintertime. John and Ken would use the barn. The chicken coops could wait awhile for new roofs as the weather would not be cold for a long while.

As they walked down to the fields, they could see they were better off than expected. The storm going from corner to corner had only wiped out about half of the crop. The big garden had not been hit, so there would be a lot of turnips and corn this winter. They were both pleased that not everything had been lost.

The part that had been hit was just level and would have to be plowed over. The summer fallow was in this part and had maybe lost a bit of top soil, but that was all.

After this, they walked back up to the buildings and John went to take care of the horses they had hurried into the barn. With the excitement, he had forgotten all about them.

When they got back to the barn, Ken was still digging his hole in the manure pile. John walked over and said,

"You're doing a good job,Ken. I think the hole is big enough now. Keep up the good work."

Ken smiled and said, "Thanks, Dad," He liked praise from his dad.

Florence then said, "I had better get up to the house and see if the girls are doing as good a job."

Ken smiled again and went back to work.

It was going to be a lot of work to try and get things back as they were, but it had to be done. The life of a farmer was not always easy.

CHAPTER 17

YEAR END 1938

The clean-up started after the big wind and hail storm, John had no crop insurance, so had to stand the loss for what had been ruined. The rain that had come with the storm helped the crops that had not been hit. The garden beside the house was hit bad and just the root crops like beets, carrots and parsnips seemed to keep growing. All the other plants like tomatoes, pumpkins, squash and other like vegetables were ruined. The potatoes, corn and turnips in the big field were fine and would yield a good harvest.

For days the food tasted like it had sand in it. It was hard to think of how the dust could get into everything.

The first thing John did was build a new outhouse. Then he put new roofs on the chicken pens. He only did three of the four buildings as they had lost about a quarter of the hens. It made no sense to pay for more roofing material than what was needed.

A lot of the farmers had lost most of their crops. The Fords were lucky as the storm went just south of them and they only had a bit of wind damage. The path of the storm had not been too wide but sure had done a lot of damage where it did hit.

What grain that could be harvested was not a bad crop. The price was still low, but a better grade paid a little more. John did the same as before and sold his grain and bought cheaper grades just for feed.

In the Spring the farm next to John had been bought by the Field family. They had one daughter who was about the same age as Flo. They became good friends over the summer. Mrs. Field was just a little bit of a woman and her husband was a big man of over six and a half feet tall. They were good neighbours but kept to themselves most of the time.

Sometimes at night, John would walk over around eight o'clock to hear the news on the radio. His battery had gone dead and he didn't want to buy a new set right now.

Florence would miss John about this time, but figured out where he was going. Things were starting to get heated up in Europe and he was interested in what was going on. Some people said there might be another war with the Germans. John had been there once and didn't like what he was hearing.

After the harvest, it was time to get ready for another winter. Everyone hoped it would be better than the summer. With dry hot weather, then storms, it had not been the best.

There were pigs to haul to market, straw to haul up to the barn and many other small jobs that had to be done.

Ken was allowed to take one of the quiet horses and hook it to the stone boat and haul wood over to the basement and throw it in the window. By letting him use old Shorty, the job was not such a chore. The old horse had been on the farm as part of the first team John had bought. He was getting old and the winter might just do him in. The last thing John would do was sell him for fox meat.

In the late Fall, Ken came down with whooping cough. It was a bad case for awhile. One night he had such trouble breathing that Florence tied some cotton batting on the end of a knitting needle. She then soaked it in iodine and swabbed out Ken's throat. He choked and spit for awhile then seemed to settle down.

Florence sat with him for awhile then went to talk to John. She told him she did not know what else to do but something had to be done to help Ken breathe better. John just shook his head and said nothing.

A few days later, Ken improved and his coughing was much less. Florence told John that she would like to take Ken to the doctor in St. Brieux.. There was enough snow on the ground to use the caboose, so they would be warm enough.

The next day, John hooked the team up to the caboose and they headed out to St. Brieux. The stove kept the caboose nice and warm They dropped Flo and Aileen off at school as they had to go right past it.

The doctor checked Ken and then went to talk to Florence. He told her that he could detect a heart murmur. This may have been caused by so much coughing, but he wasn't sure. Maybe they should keep Ken home for awhile and not let him get too tired or do anything too strenuous for some time and see how things went.

Florence thanked the doctor and paid him for his service.

On the way home, Florence told John and Ken what the doctor had said. She said she wanted to keep Ken out of school for the rest of the year. The girls could bring home his school work and she could help him every day.

They agreed that this might be a good idea. Ken was elated that he would not have to go to school. Then he wondered if Mom might not be a tougher teacher, but he did not say that to her.

They stopped at the school on the way home and picked up the girls. When they got home, the house was cold so the kids stayed in the caboose until the house was warm.

On November the eleventh, a Friday, John and Bart made their trip to Pathlow to go to the Legion. Bart and the family would stay overnight as Harvey had stayed home to do the chores. They had picked up Helen and brought her home for the weekend. There would be lots of talking and fun for the next two days.

At the Legion, there was much talk about what was going on over in Europe. Many of the vets were saying it sounded like the Krauts needed another lesson like they got in the first war. This guy Hitler was just getting a little too powerful for his own good.

John had picked up a new set of batteries for the radio. There was just too much going on to not be able to hear the news. That night he and Bart listened to the news and made a few more comments about square heads , Krauts and Hienies starting to get too big for their own good. They should never have been rearmed after the first war. After the men got this out of their system, the rest of the night was spent playing cards and having a good time.

The rest of the year, Bart and John spent time cutting wood and butchering a pig and steer each. The weather was cold enough to hang them out in the meat shed and keep them frozen. They made plans for the Christmas get-together and ice cutting in the New Year.

The Fords came to the Mullens for Christmas which was on a Sunday. The Mullens went to Fords for New Year's. Betty Boyd had come home with Helen and spent the week there and the Mullens dropped her and Helen off New Year's Day. This would save John a trip as school was back in the next couple of days.

Everyone had a good time and hoped next year would be better. With the hint of war, everyone hoped it would not happen. But it was far away and had not affected them yet. One could only hope it would not be a repeat of World War I all over again.

Books To Follow

Saskatchewan Homestead
Book Four. 1939-1946.

Growing Up On A
Saskatchewan Homestead
Book Five. 1931-1946.

ISBN 142510212-3
9 781425 102128